Dawn

Is My Crazy Showing?

You can't
Hide Crazy!

♡

Leg Bel

Dawn

You can't
Hide away!

♥

Is My Crazy Showing?
A Memoir

LEIGH BAKER

SPINELESS JELLYFISH PRESS

ISBN: 0692410171
ISBN 13: 9780692410172
Library of Congress Control Number: 2015904923
Spineless Jellyfish Press, Raleigh, North Carolina

Cover photo by Gretchen Mathison

For Dan, I'm so glad you found your balls.

Here's to the crazy ones, the misfits, the rebels, the troublemakers, the round pegs in the square holes... the ones who see things differently. They're not fond of rules and they have no respect for the status quo. You can quote them, disagree with them, glorify or vilify them, but the only thing you can't do is ignore them because they change things, they push the human race forward. While some may see them as the crazy ones, we see genius, because the ones who are crazy enough to think that they can change the world, are the ones who do.

~ Steve Jobs

Table of Contents

Preface

*H*ow did this book come about?
Funny you should ask.

I've known I wanted to be a famous writer since I was a very little girl. Between brushing my dog Jack's hair and running to the local mercantile for Pa, I'd scribble notes and ideas in a journal of coffee-colored paper old Mister Oleson sold me for only five cents, even though it was worth near triple, on account that his daughter punched me in the schoolyard for no good reason. I mostly kept to myself in town, with my head buried in a book or writing stories to escape that bitch Nellie. I dreamed of writing an epic novel, making it rich and helping my older sister open a school for the blind after she'd mysteriously gone blind when she was only 14. "You just keep on writing them words, Half-Pint," Pa told me.

Well, it sort of happened like that.

I've always had a natural desire to entertain people. Ever since I was a little girl I'd force my family to gather around while I performed theatrics or told jokes. But in 2009, as a stay-at-home mom, I started feeling a strange new mixture of boredom and courage. I craved adventure and freedom. In a bold act of personal heroism I registered for a full marathon, although at the time I couldn't run one uninterrupted mile. I hired a professional running coach, trained for five months and began to document my journey. During my training I emailed my family and friends about the dreadful circumstances that I had unexpectedly brought on myself – physical ailments like blisters, wedgies and bad sports bras compounded by the mental anguish of fear and self-doubt. I did it all with endless sarcasm, wit and humor. The emails, which were intended to be nothing more than an entertaining Saturday morning read, went viral and spread like wildfire. My running alias, Steady Betty, became famous!

The overwhelming response I received once the weekly emails and marathon were over was heartwarming. Family, friends and strangers who'd read my weekly emails craved more humorous tales from me. I received countless notes of encouragement claiming, *You should be a writer! You HAVE to write a book! You're so funny!* My personal favorite was an email I received from the mother of my good friend, Jessica. Her mom said, "If you don't write a book, I'm going to steal all your marathon journals, publish them under my own name and become rich and famous."

Though the marathon emails may have inspired me to share other stories, this book has become so much more. What was intended to be a collection of funny, independent short stories has evolved into a book about my journey through childhood love and loss, which lead to a preposterous hospitalization and sobering diagnosis. This memoir grew into a sidesplitting, triumphant feel-good story about surviving adolescence and a mental breakdown to ultimately create a family home filled with love, laughter and just the right amount of crazy.

I wrote this book for you, for me, and for every woman who has ever felt "crazy." Well mostly, I wrote this book so Jessica's mom wouldn't steal my shit, and in response to the countless other people who have told me, "If you write a book, I'll buy it!"

And to them I say, "Prove it."

-Leigh-

Author's Note

Exaggeration *is* my specialty, however, this memoir is completely true. In some cases names have been changed and places have been altered, characters combined and time compressed — most notably in the chapter about attorneys because I don't want those assholes suing me and in a few other cases where my friends don't want to claim knowing me.

Acknowledgments

I would like to give immense, heartfelt thanks to the following people:

I am deeply grateful to my husband, Dan, for his unconditional love and support. For your compassionate heart, understanding ear and constant guidance, I give you thanks. I love you so much.

I owe a boatload of thanks to my adoring children, who pretend to be enthusiastic about this book despite only knowing that "it's for grownups." I hope these stories don't embarrass you too much, and that one day you'll read this book and find it funny. I pray that I have given you a childhood filled with happiness, laughter, and above all else, unconditional love.

Many thanks to my family for showing me love, laughter and the value of hard work. Thank you for providing me with just enough dysfunction to make me fascinating, but not enough to make me completely batshit crazy.

To my in-laws and extended family, thank you for your unconditional love and acceptance.

To my best friends, I am forever grateful for your friendship and unfailing support. Thank you for sticking by me in my darkest moments and for encouraging my biggest dreams.

Jim, I cannot thank you enough. Your friendship and leadership has changed my life.

I am extremely grateful to my incredibly kind and meticulous editor, Robyn, for bringing out the best in me and, though I favour British spellings, making my words look pretty on paper.

I'd like to thank Matt, dragon slayer and wizard of Windows, for endless technical and web support. Thank you for never asking me, "Do you still have the box your computer came in?"

My sincerest gratitude goes out to Michelle, founder of One Fit Widow, and in loving memory of my friend Mitch. Thank you for allowing me to share Mitch's infectious smile and extreme act of generosity.

My deepest thanks to Vaughn and his family. Thank you for allowing me to share our story and for showing me love and acceptance. You taught me about equality and compassion and for that I am making this world a better place.

To Dr. Miller, for your sympathetic heart, understanding nature and commitment to maternal health, I give you the utmost thanks.

I would like to offer a special appreciation for the beta readers who reviewed my book before publication. Your honest assessment was extremely valuable and appreciated.

Thank you to the President of the Leigh Bones Fan Club, Alan, for shamelessly telling everyone you know about me/the blog/the book and for strategically placing my business card in airplanes and airports all over this great big world. You rock!

Thank you to everyone who visited my blog over the past several years and for following my adventures through every blog post. This book may not have happened without your encouragement, subscriptions and clicks. I'm perpetually delighted to read your comments!

Last, but certainly not least, to the mysterious girl in Starbucks who found my laptop, which contained the only version of this manuscript at the time, and returned it to the barista instead of selling it on Craigslist. You're an angel. Thank you.

Is My Crazy Showing?

One

My Kitty

One of my earliest memories is French-kissing a black boy in an abandoned garage. His name was Sean or DeShaun or something like that. I don't think he knew my name, either. I was in the sixth grade, he was in the tenth, and I was double-dog-dared to go into an abandoned building and "make out" with him. Although I was scared to death, I almost never turn down a dare.

My mother, a Southern Baptist from Memphis, and my father, a Marine Corps Officer built like an infantry tank from West Point, thought bringing home a black boy was *the* most offensive of sins. My mother would fill my head with shit like, "It says so right in the bible that you shouldn't be with a black boy," even though she couldn't produce the supporting scripture. And although I was born in Mississippi, I didn't see color.

Sean, or DeShaun, was tall and athletic with chocolaty skin that looked and felt like fine silk. He had a lot of hair with big, juicy ringlets. Not my style really, I would have preferred a tight fade. But he was cute and experienced - a combination that scared the hell out of me, yet titillated me. The boys I was used to playing with were white, freckle-faced and scrawny, and the worst dare they had ever challenged me to was writing "for a good time call Cindy" along with her telephone number in chalk on the neighborhood basketball court. I did it. In hot-pink chalk. When my parents found out they marched me straight over to Cindy's house to apologize, then made me scrub the concrete basketball court. After school. When everyone was playing on it. I couldn't have the image of me scrubbing the dirty pavement seared into peoples' minds, so I had to take the dare to make out with Sean or DeShaun to repair the damage done to my reputation. I didn't want other twelve-year-olds thinking my parents were bossing me around. Michelle was my lookout and she was to kick the garage door if my parents drove by on their way home from work.

Let's just call him Sean. Sean slowly led me to the garage door, all the while smiling curiously at me as if he was waiting for me to run the other direction at any moment. I *wanted* to run all the way home, but I didn't want everyone to remember me as the girl who scrubbed hot-pink chalk off the basketball court, then pretended to be cool by kissing a tenth grader but ended up running home like a sissy. He walked to the middle of the garage door, bent over to grab the rusty handle, and hoisted the door upwards until it rose just high enough for us to scoot underneath. Once inside, we stepped over the broken pieces of drywall and old cans of paint and stopped in the middle of the room. He looked at me sweetly as my heartbeat echoed throughout the garage. I thought at any moment pee would start running down my leg, making me the girl who scrubbed hot-pink chalk off the basketball court, then pretended to be cool by kissing a tenth grader but ended up running home like a sissy smelling like pee.

He dared me with his eyes, challenging me to make the first move. He taunted me with his cut-off football jersey, exposing his abs and begging me to touch him with his thoughts. I just stood there, frozen in fear. I wanted someone to walk in to verify we were actually kissing ('cuz all good dares involve one "verifier") so I could claim that they ruined it and stomp out all pissed off. But Michelle kept everyone at bay and the verifier never came.

He slowly cupped my face with his large, soft hands and stared deep into my soul. He could taste my fear, but something told me he was going to be gentle as he looked at me tenderly. He leaned down several inches until our faces met, looked deep into my eyes and slow-ly stuck out his tongue, caressing my bottom lip ever so softly. He placed his lips together and pressed them firmly on mine. They were like the biggest, coziest pil-lows I had ever felt in my entire life. The only people I had kissed up until that point were my parents, my grandparents (and my grandfather always smelled like leftovers and had prickly whiskers that itched me), my sister and my great Aunt Bessie who had on three tubes of neon pink lipstick. This was unlike anything I had ever experienced. His tongue was warm and wet slid-ing from side to side in my mouth. His lips seemed to swallow me up and the more he kissed me, the more I melted into his body. *Oh my God! His tongue is in my mouth! How long does this last exactly? How long do I have to tongue wrestle for my dare duties to be considered fulfilled?* His eyes asked if he could go further, and my eyes an-swered, *I don't know.* He slid his hands down my neon, paint-splattered off-the-shoulder sweatshirt and down to my Miller's Outpost jeans. Even at twelve years old, I knew it was best for him to bypass second base, as I didn't have much in the way of boobies. I knew my butt, however, would impress the brothers.

Sean kept his eyes open the entire time he kissed me, sending me into fits of desire. He was speaking the language of love without saying a single word. My heart was thrashing inside my chest as I developed a sticky coating on the palms of my hands. I felt a tingling sensation in places I had never experienced and my skin felt fiery as the kiss was all-consuming. I was petrified of being in such close confines with him as our breath swirled together creating a cloud of passion. I could literally feel each cell in my body reacting to his every touch. My mind soared in and out of the physical allure searching for ways to make sense of how I ended up in a garage kissing a boy. It was just the day before that I sat in this garage mixing shades of deserted paint for my cardboard-constructed lemonade stand. How did I go from experimenting with dirt and paint to experimenting with bodily sweat and saliva? As I tried to process the reasons I shouldn't be there, my mind was jerked right back to the physical sensation of a tooth nibbling on my lower lip. *Are we biting now? Should I try biting back?* I danced back and forth between *being* kissed and being the aggressor trying to demonstrate my own skillfulness, albeit illusory.

With one hand caressing my face and the other maneuvering through my button-flies, I thought, *Damn, this kid really knows what he's doing!* He slowly popped the top button open. *Oh, shit!* Then the second. Then the third. *Whoa! This guy really knows his way around a girl's pants.* My heart beat faster and faster. I thought I was going to jump out of my skin. This was the BIGGEST dare I had ever taken. As he reached for the final button of my stonewashed jeans, I sheepishly glanced down and abruptly transitioned from passion to horror. It was Thursday, and I was wearing my Saturday Garfield panties that read "No Preservatives" with tiny red paw prints sprinkled about. My erupting sexual desires and trembling fear came to a screeching halt and were instantaneously replaced with complete and utter embarrassment.

We had been kissing for so long that my lookout, Michelle, had ridden her bike home, leaving me and my sinful ways alone in the garage with Sean. I ran all the way to her house while stretching my neon, paint-splattered sweatshirt down over my hips to cover my open jeans and my... kitty.

And that's when my hatred for cats and love of cute panties began.

Two

Um, That's Not Oral Sex

My first *real* boyfriend was Brett. I was 14 and he was 18. I had an impractical habit of liking my sister's friends, and Brett had a job in the meat department of the specialty supermarket where she worked. He was so cute. And white - a characteristic my parents quite admired. Brett was very tall compared to my prepubescent body, and strappingly muscular with wavy, blonde hair and piercing blue eyes. He wore a baby blue Seersucker blazer in his senior portrait, which I remember vividly because I held that photo close to me each night as I dreamed of our future together.

Unfortunately, Brett did not visualize our future quite like I did. We were to be married with 2.5 children and live in a little cottage with a Dutch door in Corona

Del Mar just steps from the ocean and Starbucks. In *his* dreams we were not, um, together.

At 18 years old, my sister married her high school sweetheart and purchased a home in the neighborhood where Brett, his brother and father lived. I lived with my sister part-time and often walked or rode my bike to Brett's house. He had the place to himself an awful lot, so we'd sit on the couch and listen to music as he hung on my every word – or so it seemed. I thought he was genuinely interested in what happened in debate class that day, or *exactly* how many weeks I had until I was eligible for Driver's Ed. Sometimes he'd sing lyrics out loud, which I'm sure were directed at me. Coincidentally, it was during those times when he was most attentive that he'd casually fiddle with my shirt or pants.

One day after school we were just hanging out in his bedroom and he matter-of-factly asked, "Do you like oral sex?"

I looked at him suspiciously and stumbled with my words. "Of course I do."

"Do you even *know* what oral sex is?" Something about his squinting eyes, cocked head and wry smile made it sound more like a playful accusation than a question.

"Yes," I asserted with the utmost confidence, almost defiant, as if he'd insulted me.

"Have you ever *had* oral sex?" he questioned further.

My innocent eyes opened wide.

Confused, I asked, "Aren't we having it right now?"

One crisp autumn day, shortly after Brett bluntly and wearily explained what oral sex actually was, I stopped by his house on the way home from school. As I sauntered past the swaying palm trees in his lawn, I noticed the drapes were missing from the windows. *All* of the windows. I foolishly wondered if they were having them dry cleaned. *Funny, he didn't mention they were having them dry cleaned,* I thought, but then again we didn't usually talk about stuff like that; he was too busy complimenting me on my tan or clothes. I rang the doorbell several times before peering in the window, and was surprised to discover that all the furniture was gone too. *Hmm,* I thought. *Do people send all their furniture away to get dry cleaned too?*

Nope. That bastard had just up and moved away without telling me.

And that was the end of my relationship with Brett.

It was not, however, the end of my infatuation with Brett. I had given him my virginity on Halloween night, a week after my fifteenth birthday, along with a $199.99 leather jacket on our 3-month anniversary and *poof!*... Just like that, my dignity and hard-earned summer cash were gone. But I was determined not to let them – or Brett – get away so easily.

I declared my unwavering love for him and vowed not to eat a single bite of food for nearly three days. I thought my sudden, unexpected depression and anorexia would somehow entice him to come back to me. I was certain a daily regimen of binging, purging or starving would surely mask my insecurities and make him reappear in my life.

I cried myself to sleep for weeks speculating that Brett's entire family and the contents of their home had been kidnapped or – slightly less likely – abducted by aliens. I even entertained the possibility they were in the Witness Protection Program. I tried to convince myself that he was just too in love with me to say goodbye. It would hurt him too much.

In reality, he'd moved 30 minutes away and simply never wanted to see me again.

I guess after he'd gotten what he wanted, at least partially anyway, my stories about debate class didn't seem so interesting after all leading him to find oral sex elsewhere.

I've never forgiven Brett for that.

How was I supposed to know oral sex didn't mean *talking about sex?*

Three

BOY CRAZY

$\mathcal{M}$y mother encouraged me to date again. And eat. She cried right along with me for weeks as I re-examined every step in my failed relationship with Brett, wondering what I could have done differently. (Besides spending more time mastering oral sex, obviously.) "All men are jerks," she'd say. "You just have to find the least jerky of them that you can put up with."

What? These are my options? Starve alone or live with the least jerky guy I can find? My future seemed bleak.

I remembered the passionate kiss I'd shared years earlier with a sexy young man in an abandoned garage. He didn't seem like a jerk. What was different about him? Oh, *riiiiiight.* That whole race thing.

Eventually, I did start dating again; Vaughn was the quarterback of the football team. He was quite tall and muscular, probably larger than my father. He was sweet, funny, Christian (I suppose) and, it just so happens, black. He was the only black boy in my high school, and I immediately liked everything about him and his family. He was my Theo, and his parents were my Dr. and Mrs. Huxtable. They were everything my parents weren't and, most importantly, racially tolerant.

By the time I began dating Vaughn, my parents had had it with my sister and me and our shenanigans over boys. To them, nice, white girls didn't bring home black boys, even though I'd always thought we were the cool family when I was younger. I have an adopted black cousin, for God's sake! Debbie and I were inseparable cousins and spent every summer together at my grandparents' house in Northern California. Apparently, my parents never noticed *her* skin color all those years because she was *family*.

My mother kept throwing unsubstantiated Bible verses in my face to support their old-school discrimination, so I tried to make the connection that if we went back to Adam and Eve, Debbie and Vaughn were actually related and, thus, Vaughn was part of our family, too. My parents weren't convinced. The genealogy was lost on them and I was forbidden to date Vaughn.

Vaughn's parents were less concerned about our racial differences than my folks. He was the youngest of five children who were all in long-term relationships with white kids, so they were used to the questions, the glares, and the different hair products. They saw the potential for cute grandbabies, whereas my parents visualized lynchings and bricks being hurled through the living room window. No matter how much I professed my love for him, my parents wouldn't allow us to be together.

As in my one prior relationship, I believed Vaughn and I were destined to be together – except this time I also felt a zealous desire to vindicate every black American who ever felt treated less than equal. Quotes from Abraham Lincoln and Martin Luther King, Jr. became part of my daily dialogue, and I relished every opportunity to express my newfound passion for justice and equality.

Vaughn and I were in love, and together we knew more than my overprotective parents. We couldn't imagine why anyone cared about the color of our skin, and we didn't understand the gentle forewarnings about race that our parents spouted, based on experiences they'd had growing up in the 50's. Moreover, we couldn't fathom the idea that anyone would judge, discriminate or, worse, *threaten* us just because our skin color didn't match one another's. I mean, we were quite popular in the quad on campus, so why wouldn't we be equally welcomed in the great, big world?

And yet, we were *not* equally welcomed in the world outside campus. At school, our love was completely candid and unguarded. In public, however, our relationship mainly consisted of sneaking around and hoping my parents didn't catch us together. I wasn't very good at living undercover, though; a key element of leading a righteous crusade was supposed to be pride and, ideally, being noticed by the people you're trying to change.

Hiding our relationship was exhausting.

Vaughn and I snuck around like convicts on the run, avoiding anyone who might rat us out. My mom continued to fill my head with unsupported Biblical lies and threats, claiming I should be with someone my own race. She even tried intimidation tactics, like leaving spiteful notes taped to my bedroom door that read, "I know where you were tonight." Sometimes she was just guessing, but other times I'd accidentally blown my own cover.

I worked at a record store until 11 p.m. on school nights, and because I wasn't allowed to call Vaughn from home, I often called him from the store. On one occasion, I accidentally dialed my own house and woke my mom up.

"Is Vaughn there?"

"Excuse me?" she huffed. After recognizing her voice, I panicked and hung up.

I had my friend immediately call back and coyly ask, "Is Ron there?"

"No!" my mother barked.

My girlfriend said, "Oh, I'm so sorry. What number is this, because I just called a second ago too. I'm looking for a Ron. R-O-N." Very convincing.

When I got home from work there was a note on my door that read, "I clearly heard YOU the first time you called and asked for Vaughn."

The intimidation went beyond little notes, though. Another time, Vaughn and I were making out in a car on Newport Beach when a man in a military uniform accosted me. I suspect it was one of my Dad's spies trying to bust me, TMZ-style; my parents were on to me, and their subtle diplomacy had come to an end.

My parents eventually intervened with an orchestrated attempt to get me professional help for, what they saw as, my racial "addiction." They cited all the arguments you might expect. "What will people think when you walk down the street together?" and "Your children will be discriminated against." "God intended for you to marry within your own race," and "You know your grandparents in Memphis will disown you." They even took me to a psychiatrist, under the false pretense that it was SAT prep. I imagine they simply said, "Something's wrong with her. Fix her."

That shrink stuck out his hand and said, "Nice to meet you. So I hear you're bumpin' bush with the Harlem Globetrotters. What can I do for you?"

Um… nothing. I'm good. Thanks.

Their attempts to keep us apart didn't work. As a matter of fact, it only encouraged us to find more creative ways to be together. I tried to outsmart them all by having a white stunt double as my prom date. (There. I finally admitted it, Mom and Dad. I went to prom with Vaughn.) Surely no teenager had ever devised a plan as ingenious as staging a phony date! I thought I was quite clever to think up such a plot. My friend Mitch agreed to be the decoy.

"I'll pay for the pictures. Just pick me up and act like you're my boyfriend," I told him.

My phony prom date.   *My real prom date.*

Of *course* we went to prom together, right? This photo of us drinking beer at a party is proof. Look at the eye contact. That's undeniable chemistry.

I'm not sure if my parents bought that story, but they continued their efforts to keep me away from Vaughn. They tried everything, from bribing me with exotic trips to Hawaii, to threatening me with unplugging the phone and taking it to work with them. However, feeling defeated after several unsuccessful years, my parents finally compromised: "You can date them, just don't marry one."

But by that time, their incessant harassment had lead to our relationship's demise; Vaughn was tired of sneaking around and decided the next best thing was to cheat on me. Ironic, because that, too, involved a fair amount of sneaking around. I was fed up with my parents' illogical ideologies and furious with Vaughn for cheating on me with other white girls who had cool parents who accepted him. Vaughn's desire to put his penis in other vaginas was clearly my parents' fault and I'd had enough.

I cracked, and thought my only option to escape this emotional vice was to attempt suicide. Naturally, I first built a small bonfire in my bedroom using Vaughn's photos, t-shirts and love letters as fuel. Next, I went to the kitchen, grabbed a meat cleaver (it probably more resembled a soft cheese knife), rested it along the pale flesh of my wrist and made a cut. My half-assed attempt to end my life drew blood, but didn't do me in. I was still coherent enough to wander around the house, flailing about and cursing my horribly abundant life. I might've even made myself a sandwich while I plotted my next move.

I placed a carefully calculated call to Vaughn and told him what I'd just done.

Oh, it was official. I was crazy and I wanted him to know it was entirely his fault – even if it wasn't.

In hindsight, I don't blame Vaughn for what happened next. Vaughn fell prey to my pathetic plea and came over to my house to see if I was all right. He opened the front door and yelled my name several times before slowly venturing in. He meandered upstairs into my lair to find me lying on my bed with blood trickling down my arm ever so slightly (I managed, however, to wash my mascara-stained face and arrange my hair beautifully over my shoulder for his arrival at the scene of my poignant near-casualty). He saw the makeshift bonfire of memories on the floor – the beacon signaling my despair – and asked what I was doing. I stared at him deeply, trying to convey the sadness I felt. Then I heard a booming voice from downstairs.

"Vaughn!"

Then he turned around and walked away. I heard the front door calmly close behind him, a car door shut and the gentle roar of the car engine getting further and further away.

Wait... That was definitely not how I pictured this going in my mind. He was supposed to save me from myself. He was supposed to declare his love for me, beg my forgiveness for sticking his dick in another woman and then we'd go get yogurt. Instead, he hopped in his Dad's car and presumably said, "She's not home. Let's go," while thinking, *Damn, that bitch is crazy.*

As I stood hopelessly in my bedroom window watching them drive away I thought, *That mother fucker just left me here to die. Well, I'll show him – I'll actually kill myself now. Someone will recall seeing him leave the scene, they'll remember him casually driving away. They'll pin my murder on him. And, naturally, his fingerprints are all over everything in my bedroom, including the remainder of the burnt contents in my makeshift bonfire. His DNA is everywhere! He'll have to live the rest of his sorry life in prison thinking of me every second of every single day. So it's like we really did end up 'together forever.' I win, mother fucker!*

I stomped right downstairs, retrieved my meat cleaver (you know…the soft cheese knife) and slashed myself again. This time it hurt. This time I really wanted to die, I just didn't want to be the one to do the dirty work. This is Southern California. Where's a home invasion gangsta when you need one? The fact that I have a very low pain tolerance greatly impeded my progress. Frustrated and alone, I sank down onto the kitchen floor, crying, and eventually called my mom.

That little stunt landed me right in the nut house.

Once discharged, Vaughn and I got back together; our affair lasted nearly seven years, well into college. In typical codependent fashion, I forgave him for his fits of infidelity and even overlooked that little incident when he left me to die. I was deeply in love, though the relationship was toxic.

Still stubborn as an adult, I decided to minor in black history and major in law. I remained intently focused on eliminating discrimination, defending and preserving individual rights and liberties of all African Americans. I had a dream! Oh wait, someone else gave that speech. Regardless, I was determined to change the world. Vaughn, on the other hand, was not exactly resolved to change the world. He *was* focused on freedom, but more on his own personal and sexual freedom. He aspired to be free to smoke pot, drink and screw whomever he wanted.

In our early twenties, I gave him the sacrificial ultimatum many women give: it's pot or me. Perhaps wisely, he chose to avoid a lifetime of craziness. He chose pot – and I chose to lead the racial justice crusade alone.

Four

The Day My Scrunchies Were
Confiscated and A Comedian Was Born

Fresh out of the Emergency Room with bandages on my wrist, I walked into New Life — a rehabilitation hospital for teens in Anaheim, California. It may have been across the street from Disneyland, but it was *not* the happiest place on earth.

When I arrived, they rummaged through my shit like monkeys looking for lice. The warden may have been short and portly in her white uniform, but her soft exterior concealed an inner, hardened core. She took my cut-off shorts because they were "not appropriate attire" for a co-ed rehab facility. She seized my Snickers because it was "not conducive" to the hospital's therapeutic sessions. She picked up my scrunchies, flexed them as wide as possible and held them up to her neck — then confiscated them because they were a "choking hazard."

Who has ever hung themselves with a fucking scrunchy?

I was systematically admitted into my hospital room. There, another nurse scrutinized me as I unpacked the remainder of my belongings, including my Walkman and Sinead O'Conner tape, which played *Nothing Compares to You* on a continuous cycle. She slapped a laminated sign on my door that read *Suicide Watch* and said, "I'll be on you like white on rice until the next shift gets here."

What the fuck?

"I have to go to the bathroom," I said.

"I'm coming with you."

"I'm not going to kill myself while I pee," I announced.

"You never know," she said.

I pulled down my pants, sat on the cold toilet and stared up at her. We glared at each other with the sound of running pee in the background.

This sucks, I thought. *But at least I'm away from my parents' unsubstantiated Biblical verses claiming "nice white girls don't bring home black boys" and my intolerable cheating boyfriend.*

Once settled into my room, I was escorted to the dining hall for dinner. The management didn't want an uprising of mental patients, so the food lacked sugar, carbohydrates or anything the body could turn into energy, and the light bulbs lacked, um… wattage. The whole place was dim; even gangbangers have less tint on their windshields than this facility had on its windows. Each patient was handed a gray, divided tray filled with some type of insipid chow and an 8-ounce carton of white milk.

The dining hall held two dozen teens who were guilty of varying degrees of offenses. No hoarders or Styrofoam-eating youngsters, though; these adolescents were your average, garden-variety drug addicts, bulimics and cutters. Everyone sat quietly staring at his or her divided tray, pushing food from one compartment to the next. I later learned, once I got off suicide watch, that I could drink the milk then shove the food into the empty carton before parading in front of the nurse for my tray check.

Circle time is exactly what you'd imagine in a mental hospital: a facilitator introduces the newest patient, and everyone claps while chanting, "We love you" in a lethargic drone. My first time there, the facilitator asked if I'd like to share anything with the group — I shook my head no. I wasn't sure what, if anything, I would share, so I just sat indifferently with my head down, thinking *I am nothing like these people.* Silence didn't offer me any privacy, though; although I didn't verbally share anything, they had already sized me up. They saw the bandages and determined what I was in for. They ascertained that I was fit, sun-kissed and right-handed.

It was like prison; you had to figure things out by observing, because you never knew if what people said was true anyway. Maybe that's partly why, if you weren't crazy before you got there, you'd sure as hell learn it doing your time — which happened to be another reason it was like prison. The difference was, at the hospital I was nobody's bitch, and the inmates weren't against each other, but rather against the doctors.

Natalie was a tall, pretty blonde from Newport Beach with a secluded room and private nurse. She didn't attend circle time, although there was one empty chair reserved for her in the event she emerged. Natalie was like an urban legend, her reputation earned by her tenacious suicide attempts. When I arrived she was on High Alert Suicide Watch and restrained to her bed, because a few days earlier she'd bolted behind the nurse's station and shot-gunned a gallon of bleach. A few weeks prior to that, she tried to hang herself in the shower stall — perhaps with a hair accessory, thus warranting the no-scrunchy policy. The empty chair was supposed to be a message that they were in control, physically and psychologically. To me, it meant Natalie was in control and was going to do what she damn well wanted. When the shackles were off, of course.

I wasn't sure how I found myself in this arena, but, once settled, I wanted to outsmart the staff in their own manipulative game, too.

After circle time I was escorted to the shower. It was a small rectangular room with six shower stalls. Each was tiled from floor to ceiling and contained no door or curtain. The nurse handed me a bar of used soap and motioned toward the cold stall.

"Can I have some privacy?" I asked.

"No, ma'am. You're on suicide watch."

"You're going to watch me shower?" I huffed.

"Yep. It's for your safety," she said. "And when you prove you're trustworthy, you'll earn a razor so you can shave your legs."

"What? I can't fucking shave? Are you fucking kidding me?"

"That's right, princess. See what happens when you cut yourself to get mommy and daddy's attention?"

Look here, you fat fuck. When I do earn my razor, you're the first bitch I'm gonna shank in this place!

I climbed into the hard hospital bed in my co-ed appropriate pajamas and gawked at my nurse. Sure enough, she pulled a chair up alongside my bed and got comfortable. As I tossed and turned, my bed squeaked and crumpled with an awful crinkly noise.

What the hell is that noise? Is there a plastic liner on this mattress? Oh, for the love of God, I'm not going to shit myself. Or is suicide by laxative overdose a real concern here?

As the days went on, I learned how to play the game. I shared just enough despondent details during circle time, cried at just the right moments in psychotherapy, wrote an Oscar-worthy journal entry a time or two and even started clearing my plate at dinner. I earned small freedoms that allowed me to occasionally eat or pee alone and eventually shave my legs. During my solitude, I discovered a loose ceiling tile in my bathroom where I hid contraband, namely Snickers bars I scored from my sister. I spent time alone peeling layers of tint off my window while humming *Nothing Compares to You*, or wandering around the west wing trying to get a glimpse of Natalie.

Just when I thought I would die of boredom instead of suicide, a funny new patient named Matt came along. An alcoholic by nine and drug addict by twelve, he was slightly overweight with unkempt, curly hair and he sang hilarious lyrics to sad songs. Somehow his guitar was deemed conducive to a therapeutic environment and on occasion, particularly when no one tried to kill themselves or a staff member, Matt would entertain us during TV hour by strumming his guitar to one of the latest hits. It was significantly more interesting than watching *ALF* or *Family Ties*.

Matt made me laugh as he observed life through a humorous lens, and for the first time I realized a sense of humor could get you through any hardship. I could have drifted further from reality and fallen deeper into the depths of depression and self-hatred. Many girls in my circumstance turn to prostitution or ascend the stripper pole. I was at a turning point in my adolescence — do I whore myself out, or pull up my big girl panties and take care of myself? I didn't have tits, so I chose to see things for their comedic value, however ironic or twisted it may be. Strangely enough, living in a mental institution provided me the clarity I needed to live life exuberantly.

It was official — I was labeled crazy and I had the papers to prove it. Once you're labeled crazy you may as well embrace it, because it's not going away after seven years like a bankruptcy. That shit sticks.

My personality blossomed in rehab and that is where the comedian in me was born.

I was finally ready to move on.

Natalie spent her 18th birthday at New Life and her parents, in a bizarrely clueless display of love, presented her with a shiny, new bicycle. As a special thank you, Natalie lodged a toothbrush in her esophagus that had to be surgically removed. I guess it must be hard for parents to know the best way to celebrate with a child who's been labeled as crazy.

The night I was released from the hospital, my mom took me to a male strip club to celebrate. I could almost hear her thinking, "I'm so glad you didn't kill yourself. Let's go rub on some naked men twice your age to rejoice in your sobriety and new zest for life!" *And put some concealer on your wrist, dear. You look desperate.* I was still wearing my hospital bracelet while shoving dollar bills into G-strings.

And so, my new life began.

You can see the hospital bracelet on my wrist.

Five

FEAR OF FLYING

To say that I have a fear of flying is a colossal understatement.

Aerophobia, or fear of flying, is classified as a specific phobia of the situational type. It means I have persistent and excessive fear triggered by flying, or even the *thought* of flying. In my case, I also experience severe anxiety in relation to airports, or simply watching a plane fly overhead. Aerophobia can also mean the fear of fresh air or a draft of air, but don't confuse the two definitions, as I personally do not fear fresh air — unless I'm on an airplane, a draft suddenly appears and a cow soars past my overhead compartment. Fear of flying is often accompanied by one or more other phobias related to flying, such as claustrophobia (a fear of enclosed spaces), acrophobia (a fear of heights), or agoraphobia (a fear of vast open places) – all leading me to have a panic attack about being in a place I can't escape from.

I've recently developed a form of logophobia, a fear of words, but my fear is specific to the word *airplane*. It's common for people who suffer from logophobia to use an alternative word to conceal their distress and fit in with societal norms. I use the word "banana" in place of "airplane." I don't think anyone has caught on yet. As a matter of fact, my over-usage of the word airplane is making me so uneasy I'm taking a Clonazepam to continue writing.

Typically, from the moment a vacation or travel of any kind is suggested, I begin to dread it. My stomach immediately seizes into knots, and until I get to my destination I live as if I'm two steps from the grave. The days leading up to any trip are always an awful mix of stress-induced pacing and binge drinking. A full attack sets in on the day of the flight, with my bowels leading the charge. One shit. One beer. And we're off with the obsessive-compulsive routine.

I usually don't pack until the morning of departure — mostly because the act of packing for my imminent death seems dreary, but also because it provides a temporary distraction from my irrational thoughts before heading to the airport. As a result, what I find in my suitcase when I *do* miraculously arrive at my destination is usually an interesting surprise: mate-less shoes, a picture frame, a toaster.

My whole travel routine is quite excruciating, like a perverse scene from *Dead Man Walking*, right down to my last meal — which is usually an everything bagel toasted with cream cheese because I only fly in the morning, thus allowing as little time as possible for the morning shitting and pacing. Now that I have children, I leave a copy of our Last Will and Testament in the middle of the kitchen table for our family members to discover while the Coast Guard combs the ocean floor for our bloated bodies. I take one last gaze around my home as I leave, thinking, *this apartment was good to us. Good memories here.* After my cursory glance around the apartment, I slowly close the door and saunter to the taxi. *This is my last walk down this sidewalk.* I notice Habib's driving certificate in the window. *Habib is the last taxi driver to drive me somewhere.*

I continue this ridiculous mental cataloging of my last activities right through check-in and security. At the airport, the nervous tics begin. Pacing. Shifting in my chair. Eyes darting around the room. I feel my throat close up as my breath enters and escapes me with surprising force. I worry that Tourette's might be added to my cocktail of disorders, due to my desire to shout obscenities and random alarming things like, "WE'RE ALL GOING TO DIE!" or "THE PILOT REEKS OF LIQUOR!"

I don't know when it began exactly. Perhaps when I was in utero for eight months and my mother accidentally rolled her Buick down an embankment into a ditch, or when I was thrust out of her bloody lady bits into this world. Or perhaps it was many years later when I plummeted toward the earth from the 22nd floor in an elevator when the cable broke, leaving me dangling between the first and fifth floors of my office building. Regardless, I have a fear of all things travel-related, also known as hodophobia. (To be clear, I am not afraid of Hoda Kotb, but I do have KathyLeephobia.) I do not distinguish between modes of transportation, fear of flying just happens to be the top contender. Ski lifts aren't far behind. Ironically, I'm not concerned driving in a car when, statistically, I'm more likely to die in a car accident than tumbling from a ski lift. Somehow, I suspect Toyota has put in a few more quality control hours than Wintergreen Ski Resort.

Why couldn't I have been inflicted with triskaidekaphobia (fear of the number 13) or phalacrophobia (fear of going bald)? Even better, why not ergasiophobia (a surgeon's fear of operating) or medorthophobia (fear of an erect penis) — I could probably live my entire life avoiding those two things.

OK, you're right. I probably couldn't live with medorthophobia. Penises are everywhere. But things could be worse; I could be afraid of wine (oenophobia). While that would be downright debilitating, my fear of flying is only *partially* crippling as I still travel quite a bit. I will, however, never be a platinum member with hundreds of thousands of flight miles.

My fear of flying got worse when I went to college. I left Los Angeles to attend Arizona State University's pre-law program, and I quickly went broke. I embarked on my college journey with a brand new Jeep, a few pieces of furniture and a shitload of clothes, but as tuition increased, my personal possessions decreased. I maxed out my student loans, even sold my car and many of my personal belongings so I could afford books and food. (Oh, and beer.) I bought a mountain bike to get to work and school but that was quickly stolen, forcing me to walk or take the bus.

By the time I was 23, Dan and I had just started dating; I had no transportation, no telephone service and I was just tapping into my full alcoholic potential while surviving on Cheerios and beer.

The first time Dan visited me in Arizona, he drove from Los Angeles on a Friday with plans to drive back Sunday afternoon. When he arrived, all I had in my kitchen was a pint of Jack Daniels in the freezer and a 6-pack of Heineken in the refrigerator. He says this was the exact moment he fell in love with me. We hung out at a college bar, playing darts and drinking pitchers of Sam Adams all weekend — his treat, naturally. We didn't want our newfound love to end, so with each tick of the clock he pushed his departure later and later.

"As long as I leave in time to get to work Monday, I should be good," he said. That put his departure promptly at 2 a.m. on Monday. Dan promised to buy me a plane ticket to fly to California the following weekend so we could be together.

Oh, that's not gonna work for me, I thought. Then panic set in.

We had some wild-swinging-from-the-chandelier-monkey-sex, and *he* flew home leaving me, a virtual stranger, with his car. Whether it was my cunning scheme to continue having sex well beyond time would allow him to make the trip by car, or that he was unable to operate the brake pedal after all the screwing – I'll never know. What I do know, is he carpooled to work all week with his boss, after explaining that he left his car in Arizona with some penniless, crazy drunk girl who gave it up on the first date. Dan wasn't sure if he'd ever see his car or me again, but I punctually showed up, as promised, to pick him up from work the following Friday afternoon. Again, we relished our time together, but when it came time to take me to the airport to purchase a one-way ticket home, I freaked out. After little convincing (wink! wink!), he drove me to ASU in the middle of the night and turned right around to arrive just in time for work on Monday morning.

We frequently drove back and forth from Tempe to Los Angeles. The 45-minute flight was too frightening, while a five-hour drive at 2 a.m. after a night of partying to get back for a morning class seemed much more reasonable to me.

Before I discovered the narcotic Ativan, I drank heavily to calm myself enough to board an airplane. I recall one quick jaunt from Tempe to Los Angeles before which I chugged some Jagermeister at my apartment, chased it with a few beers and grabbed a taxi to the Phoenix airport. I pounded beers at the airport bar while waiting for my flight, taking breaks only for frequent trips to the bathroom, made urgent by the nervous shits. Once on the plane, I quickly ordered another cocktail. And another. And another. Eventually I found myself slumped over in the lavatory, completely unconscious and unaware that I was on an aircraft. Mission accomplished! Once the plane landed at LAX, all passengers were deplaned and the fire crew embarked to take the lavatory door off its hinges and pluck me from my safe place. I was pushed up the gateway ramp in a wheelchair with my name on a little placard around my neck so someone could claim me. My friend claimed me as his baggage, and in return I proceeded to vomit all over his brand new BMW.

I managed to hitch a ride back to ASU after that ordeal.

During one of my weekends in California, Dan had actually pre-purchased my one-way flight back to school, still not fully understanding the depths of my paralyzing disorder. It started to rain while we were driving to the airport, and I *knew* I couldn't possibly get on an airplane in the rain. I started to sweat, shake, hyperventilate and twitch. The tears welled up and my bowels started rumbling.

"I can't get on the plane!"

"Why?" he questioned.

"It's raining!" I cried.

"What?" He looked confused.

"I'm sorry. I can't do it," I said.

"Leigh, it's just rain."

"I know. But I can't."

"Planes fly in the rain all the time. It's fine," he assured me.

"*This* might be the one time it *can't* fly in the rain," I insisted.

"It's fine. It's just rain," he continued through clinched teeth.

"What if a bird flies into the engine? I mean, if it's raining the bird might not be able to see where it's going and it might fly right smack into the engine. You know a bird can down an airplane, don't you?" I rocked back and forth in my seat. "I'm going to throw up or have diarrhea," I cried.

> This is a good one. We don't go out when it rains, this is a real good one. I hope you appreciate this because my business is going down the fucking toilet. I should be in L.A., instead I'm in the Honeymoon Haven motel in Bumblefuck, Missouri because you won't go out when it rains. Mystifying. Fucking Mystifying.
>
> ~ Charlie Babbitt, *Rain Man* (1988)

He drove me back to ASU again. It was a quiet ride.

After four months of spontaneous midnight road trips, I transferred to Cal State Long Beach and moved in with Dan and his buddy. He was glad that part of his crazy life was over, but then he encountered a whole *new* level of crazy — because he wanted to show me the world.

He rather quickly learned not to associate with me on an airplane (or, banana, as I would say in real life). And, eventually, at the airport. I can't say I blame him.

One time, the poor man tried to take me to New York. I avoided the airport's Starbucks, because the shits had already started and I didn't want any caffeine counteracting my Ativan — which, if not switched by the pharmacist, would have me sleeping within 75 minutes of ingestion. Instead of stopping for coffee, I headed to the bar with Dan and promptly ordered a beer. My eyes shifted around the room, alternating between my watch and my purse, the vessel holding my precious medicine. At precisely 75 minutes before the scheduled takeoff, I took a 1-milligram Ativan. Hope was on the horizon and yet I was, literally, one second of unclenched butt cheeks away from shitting myself. When the flight attendant announced it was time to board, all hell broke loose.

"I have to go to the bathroom again," I mumbled to Dan.

"You just went," he accused me.

"… just… fuckin'… hold my bag," I stumbled away.

I spent my final moments in the bathroom with images of my life flashing before me. I took one last land dump while crying into my sweatshirt, then splashed some cold water on my face. I washed my hands feverishly then met Dan for the dreaded walk through the air bridge. When we stepped onto the plane, Dan passed by me like I was a stranger keeping him from a very important meeting in the back row of seats, because he knew what I was about to do. I signaled to the flight attendant and kindly pushed into her personal space.

"I am a very fearful flyer. May I speak with the pilot, please?" I asked, just like I always do.

They all say the same thing. "Of course, dear. There is nothing to be worried about." They see the dampness on my brow, the terror in my eyes and sense the panic in my voice, and deduce that it's probably best to just let me meet the pilot.

Here is a list of inquiries I ask the pilot. Each. And. Every. Trip.

- **How long have you been flying?** I don't want a rookie. I need to know they can handle anything. Like rain. And birds. And tornadoes.
- **How many flight hours do you have?** I won't accept anything less than 3,000 hours.
- **Where did you go to flight school?** I'm actually not up to date on the best-ranked flight schools, but I ask anyway. I just want to know if

they delay in answering. If they look up and to the left, they're lying! (I know this fact because I should be an FBI interrogator, not a fucking blogger.)

- **Are you married?** I should rephrase that to *happily* married.

- **Do you have children?** Follow up question: What are their names and ages?

- **How many hours of sleep did you get last night?** Preferred answer: "Eight." Acceptable answer: "Six." Unacceptable answer: "None. I hit the local strip club last night. You're right, everything *is* bigger in Texas!"

- **Have you had any alcohol in the last 48 hours?** Only acceptable answer: "I do not drink alcohol."

- **Are you Christian?** I'm looking for an emphatic "Yes!" followed by a detailed explanation about how he holds a prayer circle in the cockpit prior to each flight and how he has personally flown to the Holy Land where he retrieved a vile of Holy water with which he anoints each aircraft upon his personal inspection.

- **Did you just come from where we are going? Was it bumpy?** The ideal answer is, "Yes. I just came from (fill in the blank city) and it was smooth as butter."

- **Can I sit up here with you?** This one's tricky. I want him to say, "Sure! Have a seat!" But then I would think *he* was crazy. What kind of pilot lets a total stranger sit in the cockpit? I don't even know if I'd be safe in there. In extreme cases of catapedaphobia (fear of jumping from high places) one may feel a tremendous urge to throw oneself over the rail to avoid being in a high place. What if I'm like that — so scared of the plane crashing that I actually lurch onto the controls and send the plane plummeting towards the earth? Or so afraid that the pilot will choke on a nut that I feed him too many nuts? Or what if he has a nut allergy and I feed him nuts, he falls unconscious and the plane crashes? Perhaps me sitting in the cockpit is a bad idea. The ideal answer should be, "No. Your safety is my first priority and it's against Federal Regulations to have passengers sit in the cockpit during flight hours." I'll keep that question on the list, however, to gauge his or her judgment.

After I interrogated the pilot I found my place next to Dan, who was still acting like he'd never met me before. I quietly slid into my middle seat and announced to the real stranger seated by the window that I was a fearful flyer and that if, God willing, I fell asleep, under no circumstances should he wake me up. Furthermore, I instructed him not to order me a beverage or meal. If I appeared unconscious, that is the state in which I wished to remain. If necessary, he should climb over me to go to the bathroom. I repeated: *Do. Not. Wake. Me. Up.* I turned my hooded sweatshirt around backwards, pulled the hood over my face, directed Dan to cinch the cord behind my head, and settled into my seat.

Ding!

I hopped to my feet with urgency, as if I'd been singed with a branding iron. "What was that?" I screamed, my pulse skyrocketing.

"Ladies and Gentlemen, we would just like to welcome you aboard. We will be pulling out in just a few moments," the perky flight attendant announced.

"Oh," I sighed with relief.

Dan looked both indifferent at my outburst, yet alarmed at this "strange person occupying the seat next to him." He was still trying to play it off as if we weren't together, and I was too consumed with my negative thoughts to address him, so I'm sure it did appear as though we were, in fact, strangers. Dan busied himself with his headphones while I settled back into my seat, pulled up my hood and mumbled from underneath the thick cotton for the real stranger to cinch my hoodie behind my head.

The running dialogue in my head rambled on throughout the entire flight.

Breathe. Breathe. Deep breaths. In through the nose, out through the mouth. Dear Heavenly Father, please guide this plane safely to New York City. Please let this be a very smooth and safe flight. Please put your hands on the pilot's hands and guide his hands today. Please bless this plane. Bless everyone who worked on this plane today, Lord. I pray there are no loose bolts that could fall off the plane. Please don't let anything catastrophic happen. I hope a bird doesn't fly into the engine. Please forgive me for all my sins. I swear if you get us to New York I will be a better person. I promise to go to church EVERY Sunday. Maybe even Wednesday. I promise to go first thing Monday morning and sign up to volunteer at the church nursery. I'll try not to make fun of people anymore. Or cut people off on the freeway. Even if they don't know how to drive. You're right. I should be more patient. I really should try to be a nicer person. What is that smell? The guy next to me stinks. Oh, I don't feel good. Please don't let me throw up. Oh God, I'm going to throw up. Breathe. It's getting hot in here. I don't want to have oxygen rolled out again. That was embarrassing last time. I wonder if they have enough oxygen. Maybe just a little would help me feel better. Oh my God, I can't breathe.

I think I have to take another shit. Where am I? Did I doze off? Oh my God, I forgot I was praying and I just said "shit." Even if I didn't say "shit" and I just thought "shit," you would know what I was thinking, God. So it's really no different if I said it or thought it, right? You know what's on my mind. I'm a horrible person. Who says "shit" in the middle of their prayer? Please don't give us turbulence to teach me a lesson. I won't think "shit" again. Dammit! I just thought it. And now I thought "dammit." Shit!

Let me start over. Dear Heavenly Father, if this plane crashes, please take my soul before my body and mind know that we're going down. Amen.

"Get this fucking hood off me! I'm fucking suffocating!" I yelled as I fought to get out of my backwards sweatshirt. "I don't want to go anymore," I said to Dan.

He didn't respond; he was already fast asleep. We hadn't even taxied to the runway yet. How could he be asleep already? My eyes dashed around the cabin and saw passengers reading, napping and cooing to their babies. I was so envious of how relaxed everyone was. Inside me, a cellular breakdown of catastrophic proportions began — my frontal, more-reasonable lobe was being overtaken by demons. My sweat glands were in overdrive; my bowels were like a churning volcano about to erupt. The flight attendant walked by and I could see her face flash across the television on that night's 11 o'clock news as one of the deceased. *Is that how my friends will find out about my death?* I wondered.

When my name flashes across the screen? Dan hadn't proposed yet, so people watching the news report, much like our fellow passengers on the flight, wouldn't even know we were together when our names scrolled in alphabetical order. "She's pretty," I wanted them to think. I hoped they'd find a pretty picture of me to advertise my death.

"Leigh, wake up. Leigh! We're in New York," Dan said.

"What?" I replied groggily.

"We're in New York," he repeated.

"Oh... iz pretty here," I slurred.

"We're not even off the plane yet. How much Ativan did you take?"

"One or two." I'd lost count in the blur of the flight.

"You're only supposed to take one," he scolded, shaking his head. "Grab your purse."

I reached for my purse under the seat in front of me, but couldn't seem to retrieve it; it was lodged in there good. I knelt on the seat and bent over to pull the purse out with two hands, which sent me toppling over onto the floor. I ended up wedged between the two rows of seats, face down.

"Dan? Can you help me up?" I asked sleepily.

He pulled me up by the back of my jeans and sat me in the middle seat, then reached under the front seat and gave one generous tug at my purse. When it came free, he put it over his shoulder and ordered, "Let's go."

I rose out of the seat, hit my head on the overhead storage compartment and stumbled down the isle, swaying from side to side. I followed Dan through the airport like a little child, alternating between walking and running to keep up with him. When I finally caught up in Baggage Claim, I sat down on a bench; Dan hung the purse around my neck and went off to claim our luggage. I laid my head down on the arm of the chair and fell fast asleep.

"Leigh! Wake up!" he yelled again. "Do you think you can carry your own suitcase?"

"Huh? Where are we?" I yawned.

"Never mind. Come on," he said. He took the purse from around my neck, draped it over the rolling suitcase handle and picked up the smaller suitcase in his free hand. We walked toward the Taxi line. My legs felt unfamiliar and wobbled like a newborn deer trying to find its footing. I kept my arms stretched out in front of me like I was navigating through a dark room as I wove in and out of crowds.

"Leigh! Over here! Can you try to keep up? I can't carry you and all this stuff," Dan said.

"I'm coming," I muttered drowsily.

I zoned out during Miss Saigon and missed most of the Yankees game before it was time to medicate for the flight back to California.

"Just take one pill this time," Dan insisted.

"Well, isn't it a longer flight going west?" I questioned.

"Not by three days," he over-stressed.

I dumped two pills into the palm of my hand. I placed one capsule on my tongue and scored the second one into quarters with my fingernail. Dan was bent over, busy looking for our boarding passes, as I slowly put a quarter of the second pill on my tongue and licked the white powder residue off my palm, never taking my eyes off the back of his head.

"All set," I lied.

Being all drugged up was a necessary evil.

We made it back to Los Angeles safely and I hoped I wouldn't have to endure that long flight back to New York until at least the following October for the World Series. Why did the damn Yankees always make it to the World Series? Couldn't they lose just once so I didn't have to make that coast-to-coast trip?

Dan had other ideas that spring.

"I was thinking we'd go visit my grandmother in Hawaii," he said in early January.

"Which Hawaii?" I probed.

"What do you mean, 'Which Hawaii'? The *only* Hawaii."

"There's a Paris, Texas. Isn't there another Hawaii? Like on the continental U.S.?" I asked, full of hope.

"Did you even *take* history or geography? Do you know anything at all other than the Gold Rush?" he questioned. "No. Not Hawaii, Texas. Hawaii, the island." He continued, "Let's go visit Mama next month."

"How long is the flight?" I asked.

"I don't know. Four, five, six hours," he guessed.

I squawked, "Well, which is it? Four, five or six?"

"I don't know, Leigh. It's a few hours."

"Oh my God. It's completely over water, right?"

"Again, did you take geography?"

"How long would it take to like take a boat?"

"A fucking week!"

Oh hell. How am I going to get out of this? My stomach hurts. I think I have to take a shit.

"Do you even like your grandmother?" I wondered.

"What? What kind of question is that?"

"Never mind. I guess I'll go." I was out of excuses.

If I couldn't get out of flying to Hawaii, I was willing to go to extreme measures to avoid fully freaking out on the plane.

"I enrolled in a Fearful Flyers class at LAX this weekend," I announced one night in February.

"That's great!" Dan said supportively.

"I'm not sure if it'll help, but I'm going to give it a try."

"I think it's great that you're trying to overcome your fear," he maintained. "So, what do they do?"

"I don't know. I think a pilot and a psychiatrist teach the class together. Supposedly, the pilot explains the mechanics of how the aircraft works and how it stays in the sky and the shrink talks about why your fear is irrational and shit. Whatever. I hope they cure me."

"You'll be fine."

The following Saturday after I attended the Fearful Flyers class I arrived back home feeling more hopeless than ever before.

"How was the class?" Dan asked.

"A fucking joke!" I slammed the door.

"What happened?" he probed.

"First of all, there's like 15 of us freaks in a conference room at LAX and we're just sitting there staring at each other like we're at an AA meeting or something. It was so stupid. Then this pilot comes in and talks to us about how the plane actually functions and how it is able to stay up in the air. I guess most people with a fear of flying are afraid because they don't understand how the plane flies. So he explains all that, and people are asking stupid questions like, 'Have you ever crash landed?' or ' Have you ever slid down the blow up slide?' or 'What's the worst flight you've ever been on?' and I'm like, 'Who fucking cares because he's still alive. I'm afraid of dying. Obviously, it wasn't that bad if he's standing in front of us talking about it, you moron.' Then the shrink comes in and starts to talk about how irrational a fear of flying is and I'm like, 'Duh. I know this isn't a rational fear.' Then they haul us all onto a 747, start the engines and we talk about how we're feeling. So it's a big airplane full of a bunch of fucking retards twitching and convulsing talking about our heart rates and sweaty palms but we know we're not actually going anywhere so it was pointless. It was so stupid and a waste of time."

"Oh, that must have been some sight," he bellowed with laughter.

"Yeah, real fucking funny. I'm just taking Ativan from now on," I insisted.

Early that spring we prepared for our first of many Hawaiian vacations; Dan purchased swim trunks, sunscreen and books, while I, on the other hand, finalized my Will and stockpiled Ativan.

"You all set for our trip next week?" Dan questioned.

"Yeah. Oh, Dr. Stanley is meeting us at the airport an hour early to hypnotize me."

"Um…what?" he asked, searching for clarity.

"What?"

"You'll be fine," he insisted.

"No. I'm *not* fine. I've been shitting for 3 weeks like I have fucking malaria. I'm going to lose all elasticity in my asshole and need a colostomy bag by the time I'm 30 if I don't conquer this fear. I don't even look forward to vacations because I'm so nervous. I hate it. I don't want to go," I cried into a throw pillow. "I don't exactly like relying on the Ativan. I'm unconscious for the first 2 days of every vacation. Not to mention I'm certain it's advancing the Alzheimer's Disease that runs in my family."

"Your what? Never mind," Dan conceded. "You do what you have to do. I'm sorry this is so stressful for you. I wish you could enjoy traveling as much as you enjoy the vacation. We'll get to the airport early enough for you to get... um... hypnotized," he said peculiarly.

Dr. Stanley met Dan and me at LAX prior to our five and half hour flight to Honolulu. Dan gave a cursory greeting to Dr. Stanley and retreated to the bar to allow the doctor to cast his spell on me. We sat far away from the bustling travelers and Dr. Stanley spoke quietly and calmly about things like redirecting my imagination effectively and focusing on my breathing. I waited for him to produce a black and white spirally photo and dazzle me with its apparent movement, or say "Abracadabra" while fiercely tapping me on the forehead. But none of those things happened and he continued to talk peacefully about finding my "happy place" where I felt comfortable, secure and relaxed. I didn't have a "happy place"; I focused on the Ativan in my purse.

Although I felt marginally optimistic and more relaxed than usual, I didn't feel *hypnotized*. I didn't experience two streams of consciousness or a euphoric alternative state that made me want to waltz right onto an airplane. After our 30-minute session, I kindly thanked Dr. Stanley for his time and met up with Dan in the bar.

"How'd it go?" he asked skeptically. "Do I clap or is there a word I need to know?"

"Fuck you," I said. "I'm taking the Ativan."

We probably had a dozen trips between Los Angeles, New York and Hawaii during the seven years we dated, and each one was equally traumatic for me. We didn't fly too often during the first few years of Felicity's life, but when Cameron came along we decided to get out a bit more. We moved from San Diego to Raleigh, North Carolina when Cameron was just 13 months old, and after a few months of southeast humidity Dan announced we needed a tropical vacation.

To Hawaii, of course. Not Hawaii, Texas. Hawaii, the island. That would be the longest trip I'd taken by air and I wasn't sure my intestines could handle it.

The flight from Raleigh to Los Angeles is six hours.

The flight from Los Angeles to Honolulu is another six hours.

By my approximation, I would need sixteen Ativan.

I chose to sit next to Cameron on the flight. Partly because I couldn't stand to have Felicity talk to me for twelve straight hours and partly because I figured, if I got really nervous, maybe I could calm my nerves by breastfeeding him. It would be a bit peculiar to start breastfeeding Felicity considering I'd stopped two years earlier, but maybe Cameron wouldn't notice since it had only been four months since I last nursed him. Plus, he couldn't talk to protest the awkwardness.

Cameron and I sat in 14 D and E.

Felicity and Dan sat in 32 F and G.

I wondered why Dan sat us so far apart from each other, but didn't dwell on it.

Somewhere over the Pacific Ocean I heaved Cameron's infant carrier to row 32, bumping into each headrest along the way.

"Psst. Dan. Psst! Psshhht!" I tried to whisper.

"What?" Dan awoke.

"Cush you wash him for a minute?" I mumbled.

"What?"

"Cush you juz wash… I mean wash… CH… TCH… watch the baby… our baby cuz I gotta goze pee realz bad," I struggled to say.

"Oh, yeah," he finally understood.

"I juz can't hold it… onto it… any more."

"It's fine. Go." He shooed me away.

Dan dozed off again and awoke to the murmur of a crowd forming around the lavatory.

"They've been in there a long time," someone said.

"I think someone's locked in there," he heard another one say.

Dan made his way to the front of the line with the two kids in tow.

"Excuse me. Excuse me. Hi. Excuse me. I think my wife's in there. Excuse me," he apologized through the waiting crowd.

Knock. Knock.

"Leigh?"

Knock. Knock.

"Leigh? Are you in there?" But he knew.

I slid the latch from Occupied to Vacant, cracked the folded door and peeked out suspiciously.

"Are you OK?" he asked.

I stared through him.

"What the hell are you doing in there?" Dan scolded.

"Cooj yew git da jai-per bag," I slurred.

"What?" He tried to decipher my garbled language.

"Ze diaper bag," I clarified.

"The diaper bag? Why?"

My eyes struggled to stay at half-mast. "I forgot to pull my pantz down to go pee."

He looked me squarely in the face and said, "You're a fucking idiot" as he turned on his heels and marched back to his seat with both kids.

I stumbled out of the lavatory with my pee-soaked panties and returned to my seat alone. Rather than patiently wait for passengers to reposition, I clumsily scaled over them with my wet underwear swinging from my clenched hand, knocking people in the face. I collapsed into my seat, forcefully lowered my tray table and placed my foul panties prominently in the center of the tray. Then I promptly dozed off in my sour-smell-ing jeans as they stiffened underneath me.

I no longer wonder why Dan reserves our airline seats so far apart. As long as fear of flying doesn't out-weigh my newfound fear of incontinence and Ativan is readily available, I will continue to explore this great big world 18 rows away from Dan and the children – albeit with an extra pair of panties or two in my carryon.

Six

FROSTY THE SNOWMAN NEEDS TWO BALLS

*O*ne of my favorite movies is *Breakfast at Tiffany's* and like many girls, I dreamed of one day receiving a little blue box with a white satin ribbon holding the most brilliant diamond imaginable. During most of the seven years Dan and I dated, however, he refused to enter any jewelry store, much less Tiffany & Co. I relied on photos ripped from the pages of fashion magazines to notify him of my nuptial hardware wishes, which I taped all over our apartment to remind him on a daily basis of my particular precious desires.

I must've promised him a blowjob or something, because on one occasion I finally did manage to lure him into a Tiffany & Co. store to "just look." (Girl speak: to pick out the diamond he'd be buying me.) As I bent over the glass, the huge number of sparkling things instantly captivated me. I eased Dan into the experience of "just looking" at diamonds by admiring a cute little pillbox that was shaped like a purse. It was no bigger than an inch, sterling silver and looked like a tiny Kate Spade handbag. The top opened like a clutch to store your meds.

"How cute is that?" I motioned to Dan. It really was cute, but I was just using it as a subtle transition to the main attraction.

When I saw it, I just knew — I focused in on the most dazzling specimen I had ever laid my eyes on. For a moment, time stood still and it was just the diamond and me. It was a beautiful introduction.

I spent a few more minutes admiring my engagement ring (well, technically it still belonged to Tiffany) while Dan sweated profusely over the thought of spending more than three months of his salary on a shiny pebble. We left Tiffany & Co. that day empty-handed, but I was certain that Dan had acquired a truer sense of exactly what I wanted in an engagement ring, which would be crucial information when he set out to make his big purchase.

We continued to frolic in the flower fields (more like played darts and slammed pitchers of Sam Adams at Hennessey's Tavern in Manhattan Beach with the occasional Las Vegas binge thrown in there), as our relationship grew stronger year after year after year. In short: I waited. And waited. And waited. Then one day my phone rang:

"Hey, do we have any plans this weekend?" he casually inquired.

"I don't think so. Why?"

"Do you want to go to Palm Springs and go golfing?" he asked.

"Sure," I responded half-heartedly as I searched through legal exhibits on my desk.

That call was nothing out of the ordinary; we frequently went golfing in Palm Springs. A few minutes later, however, I received another call.

"Hey, it's me again. Can you take Friday off? I was thinking maybe we would drive out Friday and have a long weekend," he probed.

"Yeah, I'm sure I can swing that." I continued rifling through papers at the law office.

Now, that was a little weird. Dan, who was an overly high-strung investment banker, never took a day off work. Later that day I called him at his office.

"Hi, Esther, it's Leigh. Is Dan around?" I asked.

Esther fumbled, "No. He went downtown with Brian. He said he'd be back later."

And this is what happened in my mind: *What? He drove to downtown L.A.? From Pasadena? With Brian? Why? Wait! This weekend is Valentine's Day. He wants to take a day off work? For no apparent reason? Hmm… Brian's married. Dan said he would never buy a wedding ring alone. He also mentioned he would go with someone who'd already purchased a diamond. He also said he would never pay retail value for a diamond. He said he'd go someplace like the diamond district in downtown L.A. OH MY GOD, HE'S GOING TO PROPOSE THIS WEEKEND! OH MY GOD! IT'S REALLY GOING TO HAPPEN. AFTER ALL THIS WAITING, HE'S REALLY GOING TO PROPOSE!*

I took a deep breath and stepped out of my office. I carefully approached my legal secretary and said nonchalantly, "I'm stepping out. I'll be back later."

I proceeded to the nearest shopping mall, of course. Sexy red dress for Valentine's Day dinner: check. Sexy lingerie: check. New lipstick: check. Manicure: check. Pedicure: check. New perfume: check. Lots of sexy underwear: check and check.

That Friday, we pulled up to our chic hotel in Palm Springs. I was wearing my *Pretty Woman* chocolate, polka-dot dress, straw hat and tortoise sunglasses. Dan was wearing… I don't know, clothes I guess. The valet was hoisting our weekend bags out of the trunk and organizing our things onto the luggage cart when I saw it — in one swooping motion, Dan reached into the side of his black golf bag, plucked out a tiny, blue Tiffany & Co. box and slid it into his pant pocket.

HOLY SHIT! This is really happening. My heart began pounding, I started sweating profusely and could hardly catch my breath at the very thought of him proposing. *I am so glad I remembered my address book. I can't wait to call everyone I know and share the fabulous news.* As we entered the room that was known, in my mind, as the Proposal Suite, I noticed chocolate-covered strawberries, chilled champagne and flowers waiting on the table for our momentous arrival.

Perfect. Just perfect.

We agreed to exchange Valentine's Day gifts the following evening before going out to dinner. In the meantime, I was giving up lots of booty that weekend because I knew he must have spent a fortune on that Tiffany & Co. ring. When Saturday evening came, we sat down on the small, two-person sofa in the Proposal Suite before we left for dinner and exchanged gifts.

I gave Dan a Hermes tie. I think he liked it.

He pulled the blue Tiffany & Co. box out of his pocket and slid it across the coffee table in my direction. I smiled coyly, knowing that my life was about to change forever. I opened the complimentary card first and it read: *Happy Valentine's Day, Darling. Thank you for being so patient.*

I thought to myself cheerfully, *No problem*, and slowly opened the box.

Oh.

Umm…

Oh.

It was the tiny, silver pillbox shaped like a purse. The one *next* to the diamond I had pointed out. I opened the pillbox, optimistically thinking, *How clever, he put the ring inside the purse.*

Nothing. Nada. Zilch. Zero. Empty.

I warily looked up at Dan.

"What?" he said dumbfounded.

Five years. Waiting. And waiting. And waiting. All that pointless sex I'd just had.

"What's with the card?" Tears welled up in my eyes. "'Thank you for being so patient.' What's that mean?"

"Well, I just meant... thanks for hanging in there. You know... like, thanks for being patient with me," he proudly said.

Are you fucking kidding me? 'Thank you for being patient?' What you meant to say was, 'Thank you for holding, but please continue to hold.' Seriously? 'Thank you for being patient?' That's it? What the fuck is that shit? Thank you for holding, the next available bachelor will be right with you. You can't say 'Thank you for being patient!'

We drove to dinner in complete silence. I was desperate and furious while Dan was confused yet pleased with his keen purchase. We sat at our picture-perfect table involuntarily pushing food around our plates, casually sipping wine while trying to avoid eye contact. Not even two bottles of wine could lighten the shattered mood. Once the plates were cleared, we silently and instinctively relocated to the bar for after-dinner drinks. I sure as hell wasn't running back to the hotel to have *more* sex with him. Dan began to drink Jack Daniels, and that's when his matrimonial ramblings began.

"I just don't feel ready yet," he tried to explain.

"What? How?" My voice elevated. "We have been LIVING TOGETHER FOR FIVE YEARS! HOW CAN YOU NOT FUCKING KNOW?" I deliberately shrieked.

"I don't know. I just don't feel ready," he tried to salvage our night. "I feel like… like… like I'm a snowball. Yeah. A snowball," it occurred to him as he was saying it. "It's like this: marriage is a snowman. And to be absolutely ready for marriage you need to be a snowman," he alleged as he motioned to the bartender for another shot of Jack Daniels. "And right now I'm just a little snowball."

"One snowball?" I huffed.

"Yeah!" He thought I understood.

"After five years? You are one tiny fucking snowball?" I accused.

"Yes," he maintained. He saw the disappointment in my eyes and continued, "But, I'm on the top of a mountain. Yeah, a mountain. A big mountain," he gestured with his arms held high. "And I'm teetering on the edge," he motioned to the bartender for another shot. "And I'm going to catch lots of momentum," he lied, "when I descend the mountain."

"A big mountain, huh?"

"Yeah," he insisted, hoping I believed. "Oh, I just left the mountain. Look!" He signaled with his rolling arms and bobbing head. "And I'm rolling and getting lots of momentum." He took another shot of Jack Daniels. "You see, Leigh... when I get all the parts of the snowman... *burp*... then I can put on my carrot nose... *gulp*... and coal eye-ballz... and a some... shticks arms..." (another shot) "...and then I will almost be ready to... be... um... what's it called?"

"Married?" I suggested.

"Yeah... married!" he confirmed. *Burp!*

"So, let me get this straight," I clarified. "Right now you are only one fucking snowball?"

"...um... yep... *hiccup*... and I need two more... then that other shtuff... the nose and shtuff... *hiccup*..." he continued.

"But right now," I established, "you are only one fucking snowball? After five years of living together, you're still only one fucking snowball?"

He looked disoriented and confused. "Hmm... mmm..."

"Look here, Frosty. When you find your two balls, give me a fucking call. You're a jackass," I cried, exasperated.

The following year, on Christmas morning, we sat nestled up in front of the fire at his family home in Connecticut. After all the gifts were unwrapped and the mimosas were nearly gone, Dan exclaimed, "Oh! I almost forgot. I have one more gift for Leigh." He retreated upstairs for a few minutes and returned with a rather large, holiday-wrapped package. I looked at him inquisitively as he smiled and handed me the overly bulky box. I slowly peeled the red and green Christmas paper from the recycled box and plucked the wadded-up newspaper from the surrounding contents. I reached inside and removed an oversized, white ceramic snowman figure. My mind raced to catch up with my heart and I thought, *He found his balls!* I picked up the snowman, complete with a black top hat and carrot nose, and met Dan's eyes.

"What?" he said foolishly.

I had seen that look before. It meant, "Thank you for being patient. Please continue to hold."

He redeemed himself more than two years later when he finally *did* propose marriage. He casually walked into our apartment from work one night to find me lounging on the couch, waiting for him. I was wearing jeans and a ratty old, blue sweater. He was wearing a dark business suit.

"You want to go to Jake's for dinner?" he matter-of-factly asked. "I'm craving steak and lobster."

"Sure. I'm good to go. Just go change out of your suit," I yawned.

"Do you want to change?" he questioned.

"No."

"Are you sure you don't want to change into something nicer?" He tried to sound calm.

"I'm sure," I said as I followed him into the bedroom. "We wear jeans there all the time. Let's go."

"Don't you want to put some earrings on?" he asked as he motioned towards the jewelry dish on my nightstand.

"There's nothing in there I want. Let's go. I'm hungry," I said impatiently.

"Look again," he said firmly.

"What the hell is wrong with you tonight?"

"Just look again." He was out of explanations.

I looked in the ceramic dish I kept on my nightstand and laid my eyes on the most beautiful diamond ring I had ever seen. Dan stood half-naked in the closet a few feet away from me and proposed marriage.

I looked up from the diamond, braced myself on the bed and said out loud, "But it's Wednesday."

"So?" he quizzed.

"Look at what I'm wearing!" I gasped.

"So?" he continued.

"I thought it would be a Saturday and I'd look cute," I said, astonished.

Oh, Shit. I waited so long, she might actually say 'no,' he thought to himself.

"But, it's Wednesday," I repeated.

"So? What's your answer? Will you marry me?" he wondered.

"Yes! Yes! Yes!" I finally responded.

We went to our favorite steak and seafood restaurant on the beach in Del Mar and laughed for hours about Dan finding his balls and turning into a real snowman. On the way home we stopped at the grocery store to buy another bottle of champagne, but as we left the parking lot he made a wrong turn.

"Where are we going? This isn't the way to our apartment," I inquired.

"Oh! I almost forgot. There's one more present for you," he remembered. "Reach in the back seat pocket."

I pulled out a brochure and a photo of a stunning home, big enough to fill with a dozen kids. He pulled up to a dirt lot in the middle of a gorgeous neighborhood perched on the hills of Del Mar, shined the headlights onto the empty lot and said, "I bought us a house."

Perfect. Just perfect.

Where I keep my antidepressants.

Seven

ATTORNEYS ARE ASSHOLES

There are two types of attorneys: old school and new school. Old school attorneys were born prior to 1950, likely obtained their law degree at an Ivy League school, have been practicing law since the early 70's and often refer to themselves as Lawyers. They have names like William, George or Walter — III, IV or V. Old school attorneys view paralegals or legal assistants as a "Girl Friday," copy girl, file clerk, law librarian or secretary. New school attorneys, on the other hand, were born after 1980, usually obtained their law degree at their undergraduate university because they liked all the bars around campus or simply didn't know what else to do after undergrad so they thought they might was well stay on campus and go to Law School, have been practicing law since they finally passed the bar exam (on their third try) and refer to themselves as God. They have names like Spencer, Finn or Ashton. For many new school attorneys, practicing law is their first job. Ever. New school attorneys think of paralegals as other, albeit inferior, attorneys only because they can't understand why anyone would want to be anything less than an attorney.

Nonetheless, all of them are assholes.

Law offices then are, not surprisingly, where souls go to die. It's a slow, torturous death surrounded by catered breakfast buffets on swanky granite conference room tables. Plush, velvety curtains from partners' offices are used to line the coffins of deceased legal secretaries, but when a paralegal dies, their rotting corpse is tossed down an elevator shaft high above the impeccable skyline views of the firm's lofty, penthouse suite. Before a paralegal's body is disposed of, however, her right thumb, used to access the Biometric Access Control System, is surgically removed in order to continue inputting her billable hours into the firm's invoicing software program. It's often years before people realize you're dead. Sure, you died on the inside much earlier, but your physical death is expressly concealed, buried as deep as the hole in a Managing Partner's heart. Gone forever.

I remember the day I began dying. It was the summer of 1990; I was fresh out of high school and began working for a very prominent law firm as a copy clerk.

The Managing Partner was a short, rat-faced man who never addressed me by name, but rather as "copy girl." When he laughed, all of his teeth were on exhibit and his uvula swung back and forth as if trying to catapult itself from his swollen, wretched body. He and the office manager immediately approved my hiring with the assurance that I would advance rather quickly. The office manager was a tall, slender woman — likely a community college graduate — who wore fancy clothes and roamed the office hallways clutching her firm-inscribed coffee cup while verifying office productivity. She also listened to attorneys drone on and on about things like unsliced bagels and ugly purses that weren't properly stowed under desks (it was OK to have expensive purses visible, just not ugly ones).

At first I didn't have the luxury to afford suitable office attire so I wore a black, one-piece, backless halter-suit coupled with a double-breasted blazer — one with NFL-worthy shoulder pads. As you could imagine, the copy room grew rather hot and stuffy and, on occasion, I'd take off my jacket while making endless duplicates of gibberish legal documents.

I heard the whispers.

"What is the new girl wearing?"

"Who does she think she is?"

"Does she *ever* wear a bra?"

Then one day I got dragged into the office manager's office. "Leigh, there has been some discussion and complaints about your wardrobe. That it's not... well, professional."

"What? I've been working so hard. Did you see the exhibits I put together? I was here 18 hours on Saturday," I grumbled.

"I know. And everyone is very pleased with your work ethic, but it's just that your clothing has been... well, distracting to some people. I just need you to consider dressing more tastefully during the workday. You are permitted to change into jeans if you work after-hours, and on the third Friday of each month for the firm-wide denim day — if you pay the $5.00 fee, that is. But that only includes traditional jeans, not a denim cat suit."

My soul perished a little that day when the office administrator, who was no more than an over-paid, coffee-carrying babysitter, reprimanded me for expressing my broke-ass fashion independence. It was then — during my initiation to the spiteful social hierarchy of law firm staff — when I purchased my first business suit and became keenly aware that my improved fashion choices directly correlated to professional opportunities afforded to me *outside* of the copy room. It wasn't long before I was promoted to File Clerk and was permitted to attend staff meetings and eventually firm holiday parties. But I was still *staff*.

It was an unspoken rule that staff didn't approach or inconvenience attorneys with meaningless questions or chatter, especially about their personal lives. I recall the first time I approached an attorney. I had a burning question and the legal secretary was not at her desk to translate my senseless query into lawyer speak so I entered the female lawyer's corner office unannounced. Upon entering the room I commented on how beautiful the red roses were that sat upon her desk. She promptly picked up the vase of flowers and hurled them right at my face.

"Get these fucking flowers out of here! He's an asshole," she screamed at me.

"Who?" I ducked, but it was too late. The Waterford glass vase rebounded off my head, shattering as it collided with the floor. Water and rose petals littered the expensive European rug sprawled across her office floor and soaked my new blouse.

"Bradley. Who else?" she answered. "You go tell him he can go fuck himself."

Bradley was also a partner in the law firm. They had been married long before law school yet his office was clear on the other side of the twenty-first floor suite. I knelt on the floor wondering what he had done that warranted her throwing a vase of roses at *me*. She rooted around on her desk until her piercing eyes took hold of me.

"What. Are. You. Still. Doing. Here?" she questioned.

"I'm… just trying to clean this up," I fumbled with my words.

"Don't talk to me," she said through clenched teeth.

She stood behind her desk, pulled her hands up to the sides of her face in exasperation and yelled, "GET OUT!"

I scampered out of her office with only half the rose petals and green, mossy stems falling from my nervous grasp. I wanted to snatch a chunk of the broken glass and sink it into her neck like a prison shank, but was afraid she'd wrestle me to the ground and use it on me before I'd made contact with her skin. When the secretary returned from the bathroom she scolded me for entering Teresa's office and warned me to never do that again.

My coworker referred to the attorneys as life-sucking narcissists. She was right. Initially, I feared looking shoddy and nuts in the company of such high-falutin' attorneys and dreaded the day they would uncover my institutional past. In a world surrounded by cruel, self-absorbed pricks, however, I hardly needed to hide my identity; they could barely recognize *my* flavor of crazy because *they* were the tawdry, cracked-up ones.

The day I got pummeled with a vase of flowers was also the day I received my first bonus check. I'm not sure it was worth getting assaulted for, but it was certainly enough to replace my damaged blouse and entice me to come back to work the following day. It was just the beginning of a long, insufferable relationship and I was like a battered wife desperate to please the firm while compromising my own standards. With each motion thrown at me came an offering — a free bagel or half-priced soda. With each five o'clock rush or midnight exhibit assembly came another free meal or "Free Jean Day" coupon. It was a vicious cycle in which I endured countless nights working overtime being yelled at, scorned, pushed, and accosted all because an attorney procrastinated so gravely that I had to bail them out with the hope of not missing a court filing deadline. And I never once heard a simple "thank you."

Although I wasn't accustomed to that level of disrespect, I was, having grown up in a military family, somewhat familiar with the social hierarchy of not being allowed to speak, eat, or breathe unless given explicit permission. And that level of tyrannical dictatorship left me teetering somewhere between a scared little mouse and an unstoppable freight train of "fuck you's." I felt like a parolee; guarded, calculating and petrified I'd snap under the pressure. However, I maintained a very dependable and meticulous work ethic, and found what little relief I could in the clock radio concealed on my desk, where I listened to music during the wee hours of the night as I bate-stamped exhibits or collated correspondence files. On occasion, I would turn on the radio during the day and quietly dream of working someplace friendlier. A place where people greeted each other in the morning and shared a *Happy Birthday* cookie cake in the big kitchen once a month.

One morning, I was polishing a partner's paper clips at my desk while listening to Rick Dees when I heard, "Be the 102nd caller right now and win a brand-new convertible Corvette." *I could drive off into the sunset with that car. Far, far away from this hellhole*, I fantasized. I haphazardly dialed the number and, much to my surprise, it started ringing. It rang for several minutes before Rick Dees said, "Hello? Oh no, you're caller 101," and hung up. But the sound in my earpiece echoed even more ringing. The phone rang twice more. And then, simultaneously on the radio in front of me and in my ear I heard, "Hello? You're caller 102."

"Hello?" he said.

"Hello?" I said.

"Hello?"

"Hello?" I repeated.

"Hello," he continued.

"Hello," I said incomprehensibly.

"What's your name?" Rick Dees questioned.

"Oh. My. God."

"What is your name?" he probed, accustomed to the wary, skeptical prizewinner.

"Leigh," I whispered, still unable to fathom what was happening.

Then Rick Dees shouted, "Well, Leigh, you just WON A BRAND NEW CONVERTIBLE CORVETTE!" into my incredulous ear.

"Are you kidding me?"

He laughed. "No, you're the 102nd caller. You won!"

"Holy shit," I said.

"Uh... we'll get them to bleep that," he said.

"Holy fucking shit!" I whispered heavily into the phone.

"Leigh, where are you?" Rick asked.

"At work," I offered vaguely.

"Where do you work?" he asked.

"I don't know," I was confused. "Oh. I work at a law firm in Irvine," I suddenly remembered.

"What law firm?"

"I don't know. I probably shouldn't say. I don't even think I'm allowed to be on the phone," I murmured, glancing back over my shoulder.

"We understand. Well, in honor of the Gulf War, what color would you like? Red, white or blue?" he asked.

"Red! Red! Red!" I finally burst.

"Well, OK then! Hold on the phone one second and we'll get all your information," Rick Dees assured me.

Within fifteen minutes, a firm-wide memorandum was circulated explicitly forbidding personal phone calls during work hours. *And that includes to radio stations* it read in heavy, bold ink. Three days after that I was in Los Angeles at KIIS FM's radio station signing paperwork. As it turned out, I was offered a choice between the red convertible Corvette and the cash value of the car. I took the cash, regrettably ignoring the fine print about my obligation to pay winning lottery taxes or something, resigned from that law firm, and within a week I was sunbathing all alone in Hawaii. Luckily, my winnings afforded me an ample supply of Ativan to make the overseas trip.

I returned from Hawaii an entire month later, sun-drenched and near penniless. My Hawaiian vacation renewed my spirit, but that isn't to say other law firms didn't try to break my spirit again. Once my winnings fully vanished I found myself in another upscale law firm, this time in Newport Beach where the firm occupied four floors of a highly sought-after building with panoramic views of the Pacific Ocean. Although not its headquarters, the Newport Beach office still paid tribute to the firm's deeply rooted tradition of staff flogging, whilst maintaining a more relaxed atmosphere than its larger international office. Once again, I quickly established a reputation as a real go-getter while maintaining the firm's law library as well as the expansive records department. I spent most days confined within the dark mahogany walls of the law library performing research, and nights trapped in the dank basement where the firm had thousands more square feet warehousing client documents.

The stress was toxic and the adrenaline rush, addicting. I became addicted to the intolerable hours and personal sacrifices, bookended by triumphant rulings and champagne toasts in the conference room. Being a part of a winning legal team was exhilarating, even if my part was merely redacting unreadable documents in a moldy, off-site stockroom. I was hooked — just like a battered spouse. With each motion physically hurled at me, a nominal bonus. After each backhand, a pretty turtleneck. In my desperate attempt to be valued, I craved the respect of the partners, no matter how insane they were, and wanted to work on the most newsworthy cases.

As is often the case, the more superior the partner, the greater the asshole, but I adapted. I had a reputation for working well with the toughest breeds; managing partners nicknamed The Prince of Darkness, Voltaire and Satan who systematically fired people on the spot. I thrived under the pressure, worked hard and stuck up for myself with immeasurable sarcasm and humor — something they weren't accustomed to but thought was endearing, yet tenacious. Where others would shudder at their mere presence, I would boldly greet them in the hallways. While most staff would recoil in the kitchen, I would valiantly make small talk or tell them a joke. Inferior attorneys would scurry from the urinal where I would hover outside the stalls to obtain timely pertinent signatures. Most people were justifiably afraid of commanding, callous and extremely intimidating senior attorneys. To me, it was a challenge to please an attorney who, by everyone else's account, was insufferable and impossible to satisfy.

I'm not going to lie — the power and influence was alluring, too. I liked the absolute control some veteran attorneys flaunted, but mostly I wanted to be sponge-like and learn as much as I could in my early legal endeavors. I once even had a steamy make-out session with a senior partner in the hopes it would get me promoted out of the filthy, oppressive file room and closer to the legal action; all it did was earn me back-up receptionist status in the event the prettier receptionist got sick. I continued to work hard, despite being less pretty and grossly underpaid, and began a crusade to increase legal assistant salaries firm wide. Cloaked in my renewed legal appetite, poor wages struck me as a deplorable injustice to paralegals everywhere! After I successfully made my case for better wages and garnered my peers a hefty raise, I promptly quit and moved on to another firm. My friend and I boldly marched out in a show of solidarity, but not before we changed all the firm letterhead to *Pit, O'Hell & Asshole.*

My revenge felt good and it was time to move on — this time to law school. Well, technically *pre-law school* as I was still working toward obtaining my undergraduate degree, which can take forever when you're also billing 2,000 hours a year to pad the pockets of the soul-suckers you're working for. I moved to Phoenix, applied to Arizona State University's Pre-Law program and sought a job with a sole practitioner. A low-level ambulance chaser.

My first interview was for a complete derelict who handed me a prepared script, as if I were auditioning for a low budget made-for-TV-movie. He instructed me to face the wall while he made *RING-RING-RING* noises as I recited what was on the script. The hand-written screenplay had headings like, "If caller says this____, you say this ____" where the blanks were filled in with about eighteen different scenarios. He quizzed me while I frantically searched the three-page script for that exact scenario. My knees were pressed up against the rough cubicle wall surrounding his modest office; I could hear him breathing heavily from behind his cheap, faux-wooden desk. After twenty minutes I apologized for wasting his time and eventually settled on a paralegal job with an ambulance chaser who was less creepy, and even less hypercritical of my impromptu acting abilities. The law firm consisted solely of an elder attorney and his two grown sons, who also practiced law — one legitimately. The eldest brother had several unsuccessful attempts at passing that pesky bar exam and operated as the firm's bookkeeper, while the younger, superior test-taker spawn made most court appearances. Their aging father mostly napped on the tattered corduroy sofa in the dusty fire-hazard he called an office while his two belligerent sons ordered me around. They didn't have any sort of filing system whatsoever and paper littered every surface of the office. The father was an old school lawyer, and I suspect the majority of his settlements were made over a firm handshake and a shot of moonshine.

They paid me well, didn't require me to work over-time and never called me at home — three things I deeply appreciated in a college job. I stomached their ancestral oddities and cruel behavior in favor of a flexible schedule that accommodated my classes; something a sizable law firm couldn't offer me.

My law school dreams quickly evaporated, though, thanks in part to each asshole attorney I had ever worked for. While the pre-law classes were invigorating and fulfilling, my first-hand experience working for such tyrants convinced me that I didn't want to be *one of them.* As undergraduate college wrapped up, I grew weary of the small-town ambulance chaser and his extensive list of grocery store slip-and-fall clients. The dreary medical release forms bored me to tears. I craved challenging assignments, thought-provoking research and genuine exhibit boards, not the yellowing, coffee-stained Polaroid pictures I took myself of the dairy isle at the local Piggly Wiggly.

I wanted something bigger. BIGGER! I renewed my adolescent crusade for justice and racial equality just as the O.J. Simpson trial exploded, took hold of our nation and became the central focus of the entire legal community. I wanted to work with the Robert Shapiros and Johnnie Cochrans of a high-profile defense team, or grow some dreadlocks and start a grassroots movement.

I wanted to change the world — or at the very least work *for* the people who would change the world. So, faster than you can say settlement check, I left school and swiped my access card alongside the gold-dipped entry doors to another first-rate law firm in Southern California.

I got my chance to work on a high-profile defense team all right, just not the kind I dreamed of while polishing my marching boots.

Gas prices. I sold my soul to defend Big Oil. No white Bronco, Isotoner glove or murder timelines. I sifted through thousands upon thousands of documents concerning the manufacturing and refining process, trade volume and price-per-barrel of oil. Oil! Forget about dreadlocks and grassroots movements; I never even *saw* a black person while working on that case for nearly three years. I also dabbled in securities fraud, insider trading and conspiracy theories, none of which satisfied my grandiose dreams of being a peace activist or liberal do-gooder.

One of my supervising attorneys played the part of dream-crusher especially well. He consumed virtually all my time with ridiculous demands while simultaneously belittling me. He once became so angered — at God knows what, something caused by his own procrastination I'm sure — that he left a belligerent, accusatory voicemail on my office telephone. Half of it was inaudible as he was so maddened, but the other portion was a three-minute uncontrolled outburst of derogatory cussing during which he called me, among many other things, a stupid bitch. Although I discovered and saved the incriminating message from home, the next morning I arrived at work to find that my firm-issued telephone was gone. Just *gone*. I stared at the empty spot on my desk where it had existed the day before and wondered what to do.

I informed the office manager of my phone's curious disappearance; she seemed unimpressed and told me to contact the IT department which would locate a shiny, brand-new phone for me to use. *Gee, thanks a bunch!* I held a private meeting with another one of my supervising attorneys — not a partner, but rather a mid-level associate devoid of any social life, steadily climbing up from the bowels of the firm. Not only was he *not* shocked by my accusations of aggravated harassment, he admitted to stealing my phone and deleting the voicemail himself. He was the attorney-liaison between the paralegals and partners and I foolishly thought he would appreciate and defend my position, but they had gotten him. *Bastard!* I felt like Tom Cruise caught in the tangled dark underbelly of *The Firm*. I wondered if that was the moment he'd say, "No one has ever left this firm alive. Your phones are tapped. Your office is wired. You speak of any of this to anyone and there will be a mysterious explosion." My head spun out of control with thoughts of coercion and blackmail. Naturally, the firm couldn't be exposed for harassment and corruption. He warned me to watch myself. Said he'd do the best he could to reward me, and pressured me to protect the firm. There's a line in the movie, just after Tom Cruise is forewarned about the FBI's suspicion of the firm's illegal behavior and the devastating effects it could have on him if he cooperated with the FBI, when Wilford Brimley says, "So if the FBI so much as spits in your direction, you'll let me know before it hits the ground, won't ya?"

Fucking assholes.

Oh, I'll be in touch all right, but as the FBI Agent, not as the pathetic little whistle blower.

That began my lengthy application process with the FBI.

I grudgingly stayed with the firm during the extensive FBI application and interview processes, hoping the firm's new Atkins-inspired breakfast menu and increase in pay would satiate me until I officially received my badge. Soon after the disappearing phone incident, I began working for a fairly decent attorney in the same firm. He didn't spit on me when I delivered documents to him or throw feces at me as I moseyed past his office. He was actually... well, *nice*. I wondered if the firm brought him in to distract me; further assurance that I wouldn't blab. He was smart and efficient. Kind, thoughtful and, most of all, totally appreciative!

What's the catch?

Not an actual attorney? Nope. He was legit. He was too established to be a naïve ever-pleasing summer associate, too suntanned to be a mid-level ass-kisser and too jolly to be a heartless partner. A nice attorney? There's no such thing as a nice attorney. I wasn't buying any of it. Did he have a homemade chamber under his house where he made undergarments from human skin? Paralegal skin?

Bake pies with human remains?

Did he scalp Labrador puppies for sport?

Punch babies in the face?

What?

He was, quite simply, a kindhearted, hard-working, family-loving man; he was a man who, in my opinion, stumbled into the wrong career. He must have been absent the day they taught Advanced Asshole-ism in law school. He must have missed other popular law courses, such as Human Rights: Overrated in a Modern Law Firm, Constitutional Rights & How They Don't Apply to Legal Staff, Criminal Law: How to Get Away With Murder, and the always-full Ethics & How to Avoid Them weekend symposium. He was just a really good guy and I began to work, almost exclusively, for him and his legal team. We complimented one another well and together we shined in an otherwise dark and gloomy atmosphere. We worked together for a few years and for the first time in my legal career, I really enjoyed going to work — and not just to see what the lunch of-fering was — solely because my boss took me under his wing, mentored me and nurtured my love of law. I had finally found someone who valued me and appreciated my rightful talents and dedication. He wasn't an ass-hole at all; he was an angel. My soul had been crushed so many times that in my almost-dead state, I wasn't sure if seeing an angel meant I had finally died at the hands of the law firm or I was being saved.

I was being saved.

My rescuer left the swanky penthouse suite of the law office and became In-House Counsel for a Fortune 500 company, taking me right along with him. I joyfully worked for him for several more years as his personal paralegal-extraordinaire as he advised the higher-ups on contract negotiations, copyright infringement and various HR issues. And because the legal department consisted of only him and me within the business of-fice, I was surrounded by hardworking, blue-collar types who loved their jobs — not the entitled, Ivy-league pricks who loathed even the air you breathed.

It was the best job I ever had.

I stopped working altogether when I became preg-nant with my first child; then I started answering to *that* little dictator. It was one more child and twelve years before I'd answer to another asshole attorney again. With private school tuition and a jumbo mort-gage knocking down our door, I went back to work for the same high-falutin', credential-flashing assholes I'd tried to forget; this time in Raleigh, North Carolina. Regrettably, even though it had been over a decade since I had even stepped foot in a courtroom, my impressive resume landed me a job rather swiftly.

On my first day at work I was greeted by my secretary — a lovely woman, they always are — who introduced me to the eight litigation partners who I'd singularly support, and then escorted me to my private office. It was a nice office. The computer took up less space than I remembered and the ergonomic chair looked comfortable enough to sleep in. I figured I'd find out soon enough once my billable requirements were given to me. As I glanced around the unadorned office, I saw one multi-paged memorandum tacked to the bulletin board, barely visible from behind the oversized, African mahogany door. The document read:

To: New Paralegal
From: Old Paralegal
Re: WARNING!

Oh, this ought to be interesting.

And interesting it was. Well, alarming really, which is what it was intended to be. The memo was a full-length, single-spaced cautionary tale about the abuse upon which I was about to embark. It warned of verbal insults, excessive overtime, unrealistic deadlines and hypercritical personalities, namely by one attorney in particular. Old Paralegal then offered a multitude of examples illustrating how she was mistreated, at one time or another, by each of the eight attorneys. The note alerted me to the cruel and callous nature of the litigators' subculture within the otherwise enjoyable law firm and then she wished me luck! I'd had enough legal experience to know that she was more than just a disgruntled employee with an unfounded claim of mistreatment, and that her words were completely and unquestionably true.

Though time had steadily *ticked* on for over twelve years, it seemed like nothing had really changed since the first time I'd worked for attorneys. The seedy law firm culture was exactly the same; noxious and dysfunctional. In fact, it seemed even worse. The toxic judicial cesspool had produced even bigger assholes that were socially impaired and emotionally bankrupt.

That wasn't the only advisory gift Old Paralegal left me, by the way. There was a two-page memorandum in the top desk drawer, penned by the chief offender she forewarned me of earlier, outlining the proper usage of the word *and* along with a one-page account of her incorrect usage of commas, specifically the *comma splice*, as well as a printed email explaining coordinating conjunctions and conjunctive adverbs. It seems he had a sadistic routine of formally letting his paralegal know exactly when and how immensely she screwed up. None of the chastising communications were in person, but

rather he derived great joy from meticulously compos-
ing lengthy, hateful nastygrams that he left on her desk
after hours.

The other seven attorneys were equally finicky and
unapproachable, too, working exclusively behind closed
doors to avoid any social interaction or menial pleasantries. My verbal greetings were unwelcome, smiles
blatantly ignored and occasional compliments scoffed.

How did I end up here again? I thought. They say mis-
ery loves company; unhappy people like other people to
be unhappy too. Their dysfunction was hauntingly familiar and I couldn't help but wonder why I was drawn
to working with such miserable, irrational people. Am I
so crazy that I loved their company? Or did I *need* them
to feel better about my own deficiencies? Regardless,
I was there and foolishly thought maybe, just maybe,
my days of working for narcissistic attorneys were over.
Nope. They were just as greedy and self-indulgent as
ever. Nevertheless, it was the perfect place to camouflage my ridiculous ways as their antics became more
ludicrous by the minute. For instance, one day one of
the most high-ranking attorneys sprang from his chair
and went barreling down the hallway toward the elevator. As he sprinted down the corridor, he pushed people
out the way, shoved some to the ground — even tossed
his elderly secretary into a wall — without saying a
single word. He jumped on the elevator and vanished.
After nearly thirty minutes, he waltzed back into his

office, unaffected, as if his berserk getaway had not just happened. Later we all learned that he thought he saw an airplane headed for the building, believing another 9/11-type attack was imminent. He didn't warn anyone, scream or even try to save anyone's life. He pushed people out of his way and rode the elevator unaccompanied by a single person. Not surprisingly, he was not the least bit embarrassed or remorseful of his selfish actions.

What an asshole.

The *asshole gene* must undoubtedly replace the *guilt gene* sometime during the first semester of law school. I have never met an attorney who displayed any regret, shame or anguish for any of their misguided actions. They're almost proud. Like the geriatric partner who carelessly and inadvertently blasted porn from his corner office. All. Day. Long. He was "working from home" one day and remote-accessed his office computer from the comfort of his law den, no doubt. For security reasons, when you remote into your office computer the display monitor bears a blank screen while the speakers remain, unbeknownst to Tom Wanks, fully functioning. Everyone within a fifty-foot radius was verbally assaulted all day with the sounds of moaning and groaning coming from his empty office while he surfed dirty websites and abused himself for hours upon end. When he arrived to work the following day the slavish office manager obligatorily informed him that the entire office witnessed his extracurricular activities and self-abuse. He just shrugged; didn't faze him one bit.

And that was the end of that.

Like so many questionable moments at a law firm, that incident was swept under the rug never to be spoken of again. The ferocious leaders, frenzied schedule and deranged subculture all become *normal* and oddly acceptable in what ultimately turns into just a run-of-the-mill occupation. Rarely do you meet someone *so* off their rocker they give you great pause and concern. As was the case with mail girl.

She was a petite girl. Married, down on her luck and forever disheveled looking. She appeared detached and unaffected by the constant and hasty demands thrust on her, but reliable and hard-working. When she wasn't sorting or delivering mail, she busied herself in the copy room by helping the copy clerks. I'll never forget the day I approached the copy room and fortuitously intruded on her personal phone call. I was standing at a machine burning some CDs for a document production I needed to complete when she started speaking into her cellphone.

In a long, drawn-out, redneck tone she said, "I knowwww you slept with her!"

My ears perked up.

"Yoouuu de-id too!"

I imagine her husband was trying to explain his side of the story when she interrupted with, "I knowwww you were with her last nat. She wrote on ma Facebook wol 'How's my pussy taste this mornin?'"

My eyes got real big. I reckon I should have left, giving her some privacy to deal with that ill-timed dispute, but I was on a strict deadline myself and needed to get my CDs copied and delivered to a client before lunch.

"She wrote that on my Facebook wall, motherfucker!" she kept hollering. "She's all up my bisnis' and now er'body knows you fucked herrr!"

I calmly remained facing the disc burner, steadily pushing buttons and transferring discs from one slot to another.

"How would I know how her pussy tastes if you weren't with her last nat?"

She had a good point.

"Seein's how you done fucked her, y'all best watch out 'for I come up there and whoop her ass. I'm fixin ta whoop your ass too!" she hollered louder.

Then things started to get *real* specific.

"D'ya fuck her in our trailer? D'ya? Tell me!" she demanded details. I suddenly wanted to know too. *Did he fuck her in their trailer? How did she get this job* and *where, in tarnation, do you park a trailer around these parts?* My ears remained fixated on their bickering waiting for confirmation. "You liar," she wasn't easily convinced.

"I c'aint believe you fucked that whore! She is eighteeeeen years old, our son has been goin' 'round with her. That's dag-nab disgustin'. What? What? You want young pussy now? Is that it? Uh? Answer me!" she pleaded. "Bitch done wrote all over my Facebook wall! 'Hows. My. Pussy. Taste?'" she repeated in a slow drawl. "You sumbitch! You ate her nasty pussy, came home and kissed all up on me you aggervatin' sumbitch."

Not only was I horrified by her scandalous encounter, I felt awkwardly invested in that mess and, yet, slightly curious. How *did* her pussy taste? I lingered in the copy room unnecessarily for a few more minutes, just in case the age-old mystery was revealed, before returning to my office.

Later, I sat in my office ruminating. *I left my children at home for this?* I left behind cupcake days and pumpkin parades at school to listen to a bunch of asinine employees spew meaningless rubbish while I slaved away for unsympathetic and rude attorneys. I thought back to my days in that rehabilitation hospital for teens and how I ended up there feeling hopeless and suicidal. I remembered thinking if you weren't crazy before you got there, you sure as hell learned it doing your time. That's what I was doing; *learning* to be crazy by surrounding myself with attorneys all those years.

I suddenly understood the concept of a *budget* and promised Dan no more frivolous trips to Target, daily Starbucks mochas and unnecessary pedicures. Surely, if I lost those last pesky ten pounds I could reach and paint my own little piggies. I couldn't bear the idea of spending one more minute with those ungrateful ass-holes when I could be home spending *all* my time with two other little ungrateful assholes, because at least I loved my own assholes. Dan understood and felt just how miserable I was, and endorsed me resigning from that firm after only eight months.

Other than my marriage and the birth of my two children, that was the happiest day of my life.

Though I was said to be utterly perishing during the awful-lawful ages, I was, as it happens, purely existing by way of cryonics in an ice-cold setting. It left me frozen, but preserved the living tissue and maternal organisms hidden within my flaccid body. Cryopreservation, as you know, can only be rightfully performed on humans after they have been pronounced *legally dead*, but theoretically I *was* legally dead in that my *legal* ambitions were nothing more than a stony corpse. I initially fancied a law firm where the work was meaningful, the people were smart and the challenge was intense, but I stayed for the impressive dental plan.

There are more noble callings than being an attorney, like telemarketer or meter maid, but if you want to be a pasty-thighed, white-collar desk slave then a law firm is certainly the right place for you. As long as you have a thumbprint, they'll take you — dead or alive.

Eight

Why Won't the FBI Hire Me?

I have an extraordinary, albeit at times unhealthy, obsession with the FBI. I want to wear a dark navy suit and aviator sunglasses over an expressionless face all day. I want to perfect the art of flashing a badge in a nanosecond while accusingly saying, "We need to ask you a few questions." I want to whisper words like *silica*, *blood splatter* and *asphyxiation*. For as long as I can remember, I've wanted to be a Special Agent in the Federal Bureau of Investigations. My astrology sign is the Scales of Justice; it's in my blood to seek the truth.

In high school I completely avoided drugs. Sure, I might've snuck a little vodka into school cleverly disguised in a McDonald's cup — who didn't? That was high on my scale of moral offenses, though. More commonly, I might have barely missed curfew a time or two or flipped off my parents behind their backs. But for the most part, I tried to stay out of trouble; I was preparing myself for a life with the Bureau. I'd heard that getting your law degree made you a shoe-in for the FBI, and that it didn't really matter whether or not you had a connection or relative who could pull some strings. Since I believed all I had to do was go to law school and I'd be "in," I began taking law classes early in my professional quest, obtained a paralegal degree and surrounded myself with all the legal eagles I could. However, somewhere along the way I decided that law school would be a tedious and expensive process. So, rather than follow the advice of my law professors, I devised a plan to stalk the FBI.

This is where my plan went wrong.

Turns out they don't value passion and determination as much as they do education and common sense. I thought surely they would see how badly I wanted to work for them and they'd just make me an offer I couldn't refuse, but apparently that isn't how it works.

I first applied with the FBI in 1997. I was single and still waiting for Dan to find his balls and turn into a snowman with marriage potential. In my mind, it played out in one of two ways: either I would ace the FBI's preliminary exams, impress them with my sheer intensity and slim physique and they'd whisk me off to Quantico for immediate firearms training, *or* Dan would see that I was a hot commodity ~~wanted~~ *needed* by the United States of America and, therefore, I would have to leave him and our love behind to answer my call to duty. In his utter desperation and fear of losing me, he would propose on the tarmac just before the Bureau swept me off my feet. It was a win-win situation. Who was going to fight for me?

It turns out, neither.

Although I finished as one of the top three candidates, completing the application itself was a colossal feat. The FBI application was not available as a fillable PDF; I had to complete the entire application on an original Hammond typewriter also capable of sending Morse code. The form consisted of eleven pages and seventeen categories, each with a handful of subcategories, and dozens of questions geared toward retracing your life back to the womb — and if you were conceived in a petri dish, you were to state the laboratory name and location along with the barcode of said petri dish and manufacturer of any plastic devices involved, as well as the recorded temperature inside the laboratory at time of conception.

While eleven pages might not seem like much, I had far more pages designated as Addendums because the space provided was not sufficient to elaborate on *my* particular circumstances. For example, Section II, Subcategory B, Actual Places of Residence for Past 10 Years, required a lengthy attachment because I had moved out at an early age and shacked up with various boys and girls through the years, including a short tour of the southwest. There were eighteen addresses, to be exact, each of which the Bureau would presumably visit to interview past roommates and neighbors to see if they'd ever heard me shoving severed heads into my freezer or smelled strange things coming from my apartment.

Section III, Category A, Education, Subcategory 2, College Education, required an additional attachment because I took several community college classes before being able to afford Arizona State University and then Cal State Long Beach.

Section IV, Subcategory A, Employment History, required a list of every job I ever had. Ever. And because I was thrust out of the house on my bicycle at age 14 as my dad said, "Don't come home until you find a job," I needed another six-page attachment, which included more than sixteen jobs.

Section IX, Court Records, required any and all traffic violations to be listed. That resulted in yet another attachment, as I have a very heavy right foot.

And, finally, Section XII, Relatives, required a fucking interactive PowerPoint presentation.

Pay attention; this shit gets crazy.

This is how I verbally answer the question, *How many brothers and sisters do you have?* Well, my mom was married and had my sister, got divorced, then married my dad and had me, so technically I have a half-sister.

But my biological father was married once before he married my mom and had two sons, neither of whom I've ever met. He legally adopted my sister and, then, of course, had me. Then they got divorced and my mom married the man still filling the role of my stepdad, and my father married five more times but never had any other children. My stepdad was also married once before he married my mother and has three kids from that marriage, two boys and a girl, but they grew up with their birth mom. My mom and stepdad have no children together, but my stepdad legally adopted my half-sister and me. So, I have one sister.

That was a three-page addendum of 22 people, nine of which were immediate family members whom I'd never even met. When I tracked down my biological father, he couldn't remember the names of three of his five wives. My stepsister couldn't give me a straight answer as to whether or not she was married to her baby-daddy, and my half brother didn't know if he'd fathered any children. I wouldn't call it a family tree, so much as a kudzu vine twisting its way around the United States. I had to create branch headings labeled Biological Father/also known as Second Spouse to Biological Mother, Former Fourth Spouse of Biological Father and Former First Spouse of Step-Father/also known as Third Spouse to Biological Mother.

I thought the FBI would hire me based solely on the fact that I patched that motherfucker together without error. I mean, seriously. If I could piece that mystery together AND track down all those folks, perhaps they'd want me to take a look at the natural gasses surrounding the Bermuda Triangle or peek into the unsolved murders of JonBenet Ramsey or Jimmy Hoffa. I hear there's never been an official arrest made in the Tupac and Biggie Smalls murders. I'm just sayin'.

I thought surely the Bureau would be impressed with my tenacity, or at the very least get dizzy and confused, sort of like staring at one of those optical illusion posters full of dots. If you stare long enough at the pattern some of the dots change color, so maybe if they stared long enough at my application I'd change into a Special Agent! Nope. It wasn't that easy, for a number of reasons.

First of all, the FBI hires agents based on the geographical location of the office where you apply, and I applied through the San Diego office. Yes, *that* San Diego. The one with a Marine Corp Air Station, Naval Base, International Airport and Border Patrol. The one with 75,000 applicants per quarter. Applicants are considered not only based on their own merits, but how they compare to other applicants. Basically, they want to know what you can bring to the table; San Diego brought a lot of military officers, pilots, and gun-slinging, Arabic-speaking border patrol agents to the table. All I brought was my vagina. I had no foreign language skills or pilot's license. I had one white, shiny vagina and I was hoping that was good enough to eat at the table. (That sounded way better in my head than it reads on paper.)

I aced the written exams, as expected. With questions like, "If you put a dollar into a vending machine and get two candy bars out by mistake, what do you do?" it wasn't very hard. You're damn right, you take both candy bars. No one puts in more money to compensate for the free candy bar. If you said you did, you're a liar. And that, my friend, is exactly what the FBI doesn't want. Liars. Me, I'm honest. What I didn't count on were the other 30,000 candy bar-stealing applicants who passed.

Once I passed the written exam, the background check, the physical and all their other silly tests, I was called back for the panel interview. If, as a competent adult, you ever find yourself in a situation where you'd want Depends undergarments, this is it. Driving 18 hours across the desert to murder your married astronaut boyfriend counts too, but this is the next most likely time when you might need some extra protection.

First impressions are so important that the majority of my preparations were spent on putting together just the right ensemble that screamed, "I look like an FBI Agent!" I wanted my suit to convey that I was very enthusiastic, but not desperate. Tenacious, but not aggravating. Willing and agreeable, but not promiscuous (unless I had to be). I deliberated between my classic navy, single-breasted Ralph Lauren suit with the gold buttons that represented fidelity, bravery and integrity, and my equally smart, brown plaid, double-breasted Ralph Lauren suit that said I was classic and reliable, yet modern and adaptable.

Here are the two application photos I took, representing my two looks. While the outfits themselves were solid choices, the undeniable evidence of me trimming my own bangs is a colossal failure. This may, in fact, be the single reason the FBI did not hire me in 1997. My *Dumb and Dumber* portrait says it all: I ride the short the bus and I am proud.

I prepared for the panel interview exam by creating mock interviews with various people. I didn't actually know any agents, so I arranged to have a few attorneys simulate this critical roundtable with me. While helpful, the pressure of that forum proved to be utterly insignificant compared to the real thing.

I arrived early in my navy, single-breasted suit, carrying a briefcase containing my application, family tree binder, legal pad and American Flag pen for taking notes. I was promptly escorted to a room that contained industrial grade cabinets and badly upholstered rose-colored chairs. I sat patiently, examining the room and all its contents, hoping my office would be decorated in a more modern style than what was in front of me. I wondered if it was a test like in my college forensics course, where they simulated a robbery; a random person ran into the class, stole a backpack and ran out, after which we were asked to write down as many details about what we'd witnessed as we could remember. *Was the suspect black or white? Tall or short? Hooded sweatshirt or jacket?* Each detail swirled around in your head somewhere between reality and perception. However, feeling prepared by that prior experience, I examined the interview room in case I was whisked off and asked to recount the details of the first room. I studied the metal blinds (approximately one inch thick), the smoky blue carpet (Berber, circa 1976), eight chairs in total, the FBI emblem on the wall, fire escape route posted approximately four inches to the left of the door. I was peeking under the table to see if we were being recorded when I heard a "Hello" come from above my head.

"Oh! Hi!" I jumped up. I extended my hand to greet an elder, portly Agent. My shake was firm. Perhaps a little too firm.

"Thank you for coming in today," he said. "Any trouble finding the office?"

"No. Not at all," I asserted. After all, I had done three drive-bys and one dry run during similar traffic hours. The dry run was actually a full dress rehearsal in the event they saw me loitering around the parking lot and wanted to pull me in for questioning.

"Well, your written exams were very impressive and, as you know, you have passed the preliminary tests allowing you to advance to the next phase of the interview process to become a Special Agent with the Federal Bureau of Investigations," he explained. "I've invited two other Special Agents to join us this morning and they should be here shortly."

"Great! I can't wait!" I beamed. *No Fear. OK. Calm down.*

Two other agents promptly entered the room, each wearing a navy, understated single-breasted suit. We exchanged pleasantries. One appeared Hispanic and the other was a white female. *Great, we're all minorities!* They didn't look too intimidating. OK, yes they did. They had badges and guns on their waistbands. And I wanted one.

It's hard to identify which nervous habit emerged first. I'm not one to fidget or bite my nails. I don't nervously tap the table with a pen or cross my legs and shake my foot uncontrollably. I do, however, have a tendency to get very loud and overly confident. In some situations that's fine, say in a bar while trying to hit on someone. But in other situations, like the most important interview of your entire life, it's just downright inappropriate. When I get nervous, sometimes I also forget to blink. So the combination of not blinking and screaming my enthusiasm, all while pounding the desk with my fist, yelling, "*I. WANT. THIS. JOB.*" might have come across as rather belligerent. I usually manage to hide my insecurities by overcompensating with conviction and confidence; it's a slippery slope, but has gotten me every job I've ever interviewed for. Except this one.

I insisted that I was not only capable, but also perfect for the job. I recounted a time when I was in college and saw a man photocopying checks at a local Kinko's. He very purposefully photocopied dozens of checks by picking each one up between the knuckles of his first and second finger, putting them on the glass, pressing the copy button with his knuckle, flipping them over (again, with his knuckles) and copying the back. Each time, he was careful not to touch anything with his fingers. It was obvious to me this was a major white-collar counterfeit operation unfolding right in front of my eyes. Who copies checks without touching them? Someone who doesn't want his or her fingerprints on anything, that's who. I lurked around the Kinko's until he was done, and followed him out to his car to jot down his license plate number. It just so happened that I had an FBI Agent guest speaker in one of my law classes that day, so I promptly gave him the evidence he needed to make the bust. He seemed very intrigued and thanked me for my civil duty. I asked if he needed help cracking the case, but he said he could take care of it. I don't know if the panel interview was impressed by that story, but they looked like they were.

The agents volleyed questions at me about why I wanted to work for the Bureau, what, specifically, I was interested in and, most importantly, was I willing to move *anywhere* they sent me. *Of course* I was willing to move anywhere they sent me. Shit, it's not like Dan was holding me back. I mean, I was partly testing Dan to see if he'd beg me to stay, but the truth was I'd have gone anywhere the FBI wanted me to go. That's the deal and you know that going into it, though I'm sure some applicants blindly apply and hope the Bureau will place them in a reasonable location. Rumor has it that the Bureau asks you to rank your desired cities, and then they give you your least appealing assignment. Word on the street was that no one wanted New York City. I, on the other hand, was obsessed with NYC and would have listed that as my number one spot. That presented me with a quandary: should I actually put NYC as number one, or should I play mind games with them and put it as my least appealing city with the assumption they'd give me my last choice? It was complicated and it wasn't in my nature to lie, so I couldn't quite follow along in my head with that strategy. They casually asked where I'd like to go and I blurted out, "New York City!"

They were intrigued and said, "No one wants New York. You may get hired for that reason alone." *Sweet! I'm in! Let's wrap this up and get me a badge and gun.* I figured that's where all the action was, and I wanted in. Well, except for all the murder. I was mostly interested in white-collar crime, thus my keen observation at Kinko's. I didn't want to see dead bodies.

I learned that about myself during a two-week class in college called Prison Systems, in which we boarded a bus and toured 19 different prisons across California. We started at the Juvenile Detention Facility, your average criminal's likely introduction to the justice system, and ended with the L.A. County Coroner's Office, their inevitable end destination. During the coroner's visit, we saw coolers full of bodies with toe tags, rooms with unidentified persons, and stood in the examination room where O.J.'s beloved Nicole Simpson was examined. We had to watch an autopsy, but I stood as far back as I could to avoid actually seeing the body, my back against the wall under a giant bug zapper. During the exam, a massive bug flew into the zapper sending a *ZAP! ZAP! ZAP!* pulsating through my body that sent me running from the autopsy room, screaming and shaking. I sat on the bus crying for the remainder of that stop.

I figured out that interrogation and investigation were more my thing, thanks to that same class. During a visit to the Women's State Prison in Fonterra, I interviewed a modest woman named Brenda who received life without the possibility of parole for killing her husband. She claimed he had physically abused her for years before she gained the courage to leave him. Once gone, he came over to her apartment in the middle of the night completely intoxicated and belligerently attacked her. In self-defense, she cracked him over the head with a wine bottle and fled. Unfortunately for him, and her too I guess, he had a brain hemorrhage, bled out and died. Poor thing. She got life for that. That's exactly what's wrong with our Justice System. She needed a pen pal and confidant. Someone who would fight for her. Two semesters later, I was taking a law class and we were discussing clemency laws designed to protect domestic violence victims. I raised my hand to ask my law professor about Brenda's circumstances.

Another student had interviewed her during the previous Prison Systems class and said, "Did you obtain the police report on Brenda's case?"

"No, but she told me what happened," I maintained. "It was clearly domestic violence. Her husband beat her for over 20 years. It's not her fault he had a brain hemorrhage and died."

"Her husband was a Police Chief. He never laid a finger on her. She stabbed him in the heart 16 times while he was asleep one night," my fellow law student pronounced.

"She lied to me?" I gasped. *How dare she? That bitch lied to me!*

The class erupted in laughter. I was crushed. My head began to swirl.

"What about Peter from the State Prison in Chino?" I wondered out loud. He'd told me about a drug deal gone bad; when the smoke cleared he was the only one standing, and he got pinned for the whole thing. I knew drugs were bad, but I felt sorry for him that he got life without parole for that one. Wait — was that not true either?

"Peter concocted a very large drug scam where he arranged to have a rather substantial transaction take place on the Long Beach Pier. Prior to the night of the transaction, he dug a six-foot deep hole in the middle of the woods. Went to the drug deal, shot everyone there, dragged them out to the woods to bury the bodies and kept the drugs and money for himself. One victim survived, crawled out of his grave and testified against him in court," my professor explained.

What the fuck? He's such a liar!

"And Tyrone at the Juvenile Detention Center?" I mumbled.

"No. He really was born a crack baby and has had a life of crime stealing cars. He didn't have a chance," my professor said.

I couldn't believe every one of those inmates lied to me. *Why would they do that? It's not like they were going anywhere. What did I care if they murdered people? Why wouldn't they just tell me the truth?* Because they'd already read every book in the prison library, didn't have cable and had nothing better to do than fuck with some gullible white girl from Cal State Long Beach — that's why.

Fuckers.

I replayed those conversations over and over in my mind. It was then that I began to question everyone and everything; that was my initiation into the justice system and became the new benchmark for my interactions with people and view of the world around me. I already had a skewed view of the world and believed everyone was just out for themselves, but I began to look at *everything* with a sneaky suspicion, making the FBI the perfect place for me. Every abandoned backpack was a bomb, every unshaven man a terrorist, every van a lurking pedophile. Each suspense movie I saw was just a test. "I can see exactly where this is going," I would annoyingly say. And, sure enough, I'd solve another mystery before the movie was over. The FBI was the clear career choice for my talents and that panel interview meant the world to me.

After the interview, I promptly sent each Agent a handwritten thank you note on American Flag stationary. Twice. I considered hand-delivering them, but at the advice of Dan I mailed them instead (in retrospect, I see he was probably sabotaging me). I nearly baked them an apple pie, but I knew security would question my motives and possibly make me take a bite of it to prove it wasn't poisoned, and I didn't want to present them with a pie that had one sliver eaten out of it. I mean, *that* would be weird.

Months later, I received the rejection letter claiming they would keep my application on file, but if I acquired any new skills — say a doctorate, law degree or became fluent in a middle eastern language — I should supplement my application immediately. But what about bringing my nice, shiny vagina to the table? I thought they wanted more women in the FBI? I had a pretty fearless vagina, but in this particular instance it didn't do me any good.

I began stalking the FBI once I was officially rejected from employment. I spent hours on their website reviewing the FBI's 10 Most Wanted profiles. I figured if I stumbled upon one of those felons, I would only hand over the necessary information to locate him if they made me a job offer. Kind of like a hostage negotiation, except I was the good guy holding the bad guy hostage in exchange for a job with the FBI.

It made perfect sense in my mind.

Around 1999, I was in Washington, D.C. on a family vacation. While everyone else was wasting their time at the Smithsonian, I took the tour of the FBI headquarters. I stood in line for nearly three hours devising a plan to gain access to the evidence room. While others wondered around reading the historical facts, I peered through windows and under doors trying to get a peek at the real action. They didn't appreciate that. There was one part of the tour when everyone was paraded in front of a window that overlooked the ballistics room. They were comparing the striations of bullets and I yelled out, "SILICA!" Everyone looked at me strangely. But I knew.

Anytime I learned that someone's neighbor or friend or cousin was in the Bureau, I would bombard them with questions and ask them to share stories from the inside. Once I learned there was an agent living four streets over, I begged Dan to invite him over for poker. I heard the guy's wife was a Federal Marshall, and I envisioned us all sipping expensive wine together and talking about caseloads, perps and highly confidential information. Dan was not equally resolved to embark on a friendship with federal agents, presumably just in case he scored some weed, but I knew that was the crowd I was meant to mingle with.

"I've never even seen that guy before," Dan said. "I'm not walking up to his door and asking him to come over for poker."

"I'll do it!" I shrieked.

"I know you will. That's what I'm afraid of," he said.

I bought a dog so I could start walking it over by his house. One day I made Felicity ride her bike over there with me, because I thought it might seem weird that I kept loitering outside his home. We came to a very slow crawl at the end of his driveway and Felicity saw a snake, dropped her bike and ran away screaming. I was stuck in his front yard with two bikes and a crying kid making a complete spectacle.

"Felicity! Grab your bike!" I yelled through clenched teeth. "Don't embarrass me! I'm trying to get a job here!"

After months of stalking his street, I finally met him. I introduced myself to Mr. FBI Agent as a Stay-at-Home Mom 1997 Bureau Applicant. I wanted him to know I was a harmless soccer mom but, *wink-wink*, also a badge-toting badass. In theory, that is. He shared with me, in confidence, that his Federal Marshall wife was pregnant with their first child. I immediately offered to help her with lactation, at which point he slowly backed away from me. I mean, I did nurse two children to a very plump respectable weight, and it's not like I was going to start feeling up her tits on the first meeting. Maybe. Regardless, he was obviously intimidated by me and did not accept our invitations to poker or Lamaze classes. He was probably one of those accountant type FBI agents anyway, not the door-busting type of agent. Nonetheless, when I met agents from then on I dropped his name like we were old friends, but I'd quickly follow up with, "But don't ask him about me. Technically we met in a doctor's office. You know, HIPPA laws and such, so he won't admit to knowing me."

Since I was too lazy to attend Law School or learn Arabic, I was never able to supplement my application in any significant way. I did send follow-up letters, on American Flag stationary, to the Bureau for several years following my interview just to ensure that my application was, in fact, still "on file." Unfortunately, without any new pertinent material, there was really no need for me to reapply. Plus, although my vagina was hire-worthy, the Bureau went on a hiring freeze for much of the early 2000s and at that point, I had two babies and ~~shouldn't~~ couldn't leave them. I tried to accept the fact that I was not going to be a Special Agent, and began to pursue a position as a Professional Staff. With twelve years experience as a paralegal, surely I could be someone's assistant in the FBI. But, as you'd expect, there are rarely any Professional Staff positions open in the Raleigh, North Carolina office.

On my 37th birthday, I cried myself to sleep as all my dreams and aspirations of becoming an agent were officially over — I had finally reached the cut-off age. I lied in bed as the clock neared midnight and said to Dan, "Well, unless they call in the next ten minutes, I guess it's over."

"Unless who calls in the next ten minutes?" he questioned.

"The FBI, you idiot! You have to be hired as an agent prior to your 37th birthday! I can never be an agent now!"

"What are you talking about?" he said.

"You don't even know me!" I screamed. I watched the clock tick away until midnight and then rolled over and cried myself to sleep.

Though my days are not filled with dangerously chasing perps, I exercise my razor sharp investigative skills in other purposeful ways. Instead of hunting down criminals, I track down mateless socks. Rather than dust *for* fingerprints, I actually dust fingerprints. Although scrutinizing bank accounts looking for fraudulent activity would be thrilling, I peruse my child's cell phone for inappropriate language. Don't underestimate that skill; decoding text messages takes a keen awareness. So while the life of an FBI Agent would be an exhilarating rush of adrenaline, I am happy with where my life has ended up; in the suburbs. I am a stay-at-home, SUV driving, coffee toting, chaperoning class mom who wears yoga pants and a beat up ol' FBI hat every day and if, by chance, someone asks my son if his mom is an FBI agent he indulges me and erroneously says yes.

Then we exchange a look and a wink. He gets me. He's very intuitive like that.

He'll make a good FBI Agent someday.

Nine

I Should Buy a Parrot

and a Funeral Home

Since the FBI didn't hire me, there was only one thing left to do. Get high!

I'm not going to reveal the identity of my dealer. Well, mainly because there was only one time when I *really* smoked, and I don't think that qualifies as me having a dealer per se, just a guy who happened to get me high. Anyway, from what I understand, *he's* not the dealer. He has another guy who's the dealer. Duh. Maybe there's a runner too. I don't actually know how all this works. What I do know is that I was heartbroken over my years spent being a goody-goody in preparation for becoming a federal agent, and felt like I'd missed out on one of the biggest rites of passage as a teenager.

It seemed like every time I hung out drinking with my husband and friends, they all took a little stroll down memory lane recounting stories of getting high, laughin' and chillin' in the bathroom while shoving towels under the door crack to hide the smell from their parents, or getting high in the car and then driving up to a Taco Bell drive-through, blowing smoke into the window and laughing their asses off. Dan always lit up (no pun intended) when he fondly spoke of the four-foot tall creation of a bong he and his brothers made in high school. Or was it elementary school?

Either way, there seemed to be a cool club — and I wasn't a part of it. By the time I turned 40, I was way overdue to get baked. (Stoned? High? I wasn't even sure which term to use.) I was sick of being morally decent and I wanted to give the FBI a big, fat "FU," so I figured I needed to score some marijuana, or weed, or bud, or reefer, or whatever the cool kids were calling it. But I also needed to be a lot more successful at using it than I was during my first few naive encounters with "the doobage."

Back when Dan and I first began dating, we went to a Van Morrison and Bob Dylan concert in Laguna Beach. It was Dan's choice of music — my first concert was Milli Vanilli opening for The Beastie Boys.

Proof that I went to a Milli Vanilli concert.
You can blame it on the rain.

Dan and I had awesome seats; three rows back from the stage in front of the enormous speakers. As Bob Dylan plucked away on his guitar, I began to smell something funny. I clapped like a ferocious sea lion, and just as the music went silent I screamed at the top of my lungs, "DAN! I THINK HE'S JUST GETTING WARMED UP CUZ I CAN SMELL THE SPEAKERS BURNING!" Virtually everyone around us looked at me, horrified.

Of course they weren't nearly as horrified as Dan, who hissed, "That's weed, you idiot!" At least no one was concerned for their anonymity or the safety of their stash, because I was obviously too stupid to be a nark. Dan knew I was too big of a pussy to actually smoke the stuff, so he said I needed a contact high — whatever *that* was. He explained that in high school they'd pile a bunch of people in a car so the stoners could blow pot smoke around in circles, while the kids who were too afraid to actually take a hit got a contact high just from breathing in the clouds of smoke. But even that scared me; I couldn't do it.

My next experience with "the ganja" came three years later; I was at least tempted to try it this time, but it was still an abysmal failure. We were at an Allman Brothers concert tailgating (Dan's music choice again), and as usual, all our friends started reminiscing about the glory days of listening to music in a cold basement somewhere while toking and baking and ghosting through their adolescence. I listened in, and learned that I needed to get my hands on some dank (good weed), not shwag (shit weed), take a power hit, or get a resin hit if I was feeling particularly adventurous. Oh, and don't Bogart the bowl.

The more we drank and belted out *Ramblin' Man* and *Midnight Rider*, the funnier their stories sounded and the more envious I became. I'm not even sure the stories were funny, so much as they were comforting. Each story gave me a feeling of relaxation and euphoria sprinkled with a humorous outlook on life. Things that weren't funny became funny — Mom's meatloaf was fucking hysterical and rainbows were, like, awesome. Suddenly *I* wanted to laugh at meatloaf, too, and drive my car around in circles for 25 minutes watching squirrels play out their very own episode of *The Amazing Race*.

When we arrived at the concert we shook out our blanket and claimed some real estate in the grass area. My friend Linda immediately whispered, "I'm gonna get you high."

I started to panic. *Really? Where? How do you know there will even be anyone here smoking the marijuana? Where will we find these marijuanaians? I don't know how much cash I brought. Do they take credit? Do I have to blow anyone if I don't have money? My head is swirling. I don't like my new druggy lifestyle. What if we get caught? I don't want to spend the rest of my life in jail. I'm too cute for jail. I'm very rapable.*

Oblivious, Dan said, "First round is on me," and proceeded to the nearest beer tent.

Linda stood up and set her eyes on some greasy-haired punk sitting about four rows in front of us. She marched right up to him, exchanged a few words, turned towards me and waved me down.

Who me? I looked around. *Now? Right now? Do I need my purse? Chapstick? Holy shit!* I staggered down the four rows; Linda took a joint out of the guy's hand, placed it in mine and said, "Inhale." I placed the joint in my mouth and nervously tried to inhale, wide-eyed, while attempting to look cool.

Dan returned from the bar double-fisted with beer and approached Linda, the greasy-haired guy and me.

"What the FUCK are *you* doing?" he said to me.

I freaked out. I threw the joint on the ground and ran as fast I could. I didn't know where I was running exactly, I just wanted to get out of there before the cops showed up. I soon found myself perched behind a bush outside the perimeter of the concert arena, so I crawled into the bush and started crying. I could hear the faint sounds of the Allman Brothers from where I sat. Dan and Linda roamed around the concert venue for over two hours looking for me; I heard them yell my name occasionally as they rounded the corner. I was too ashamed, however, to move or respond. I just sat hopelessly crying about the awful, awful turn my life had taken.

What if the FBI finds out? What if they don't hire me because I've done drugs? From now on, I'll have to check the "yes" box adjacent to "Have you ever done drugs?" on job applications. I tried the marijuana. I'm so disappointed in myself. I'll never be able to look in the mirror again. I can never forgive myself for this heinous act. I am a druggy. I should get help. What if I get drug tested at work tomorrow? OMG! What if that joint was laced with something? What if that was some skank pot that I smoked? My lungs hurt! I'm getting itchy! I'm going to die! I think I just overdosed. I see the bright light. I can't hear the music anymore...

"I FOUND HER!" Dan shouted. "Where the FUCK have you been?" he yelled at me.

I whimpered what I assumed were my last words. "I can't hear the music anymore."

"Because the concert has been over for 45 fucking minutes, Leigh!" he shouted. "We've been looking everywhere for you!"

I snapped to. "I'm not dead?"

"No, you're not dead. What the fuck is wrong with you? We've been looking for you for over two hours! Where the fuck have you been?" he said.

"Here. In the bushes," I admitted.

"Oh my God! There you are!" Linda screamed running towards me. "Are you OK?"

"She's been right here in the fucking bushes the whole time," Dan accused. He turned to me, "Get in the fucking car."

"I'll call you tomorrow," I mumbled to Linda.

We had a two-hour drive from Laguna Beach back to our apartment in Hermosa Beach. It was a very quiet ride. Finally Dan spoke.

"Why didn't you just tell me if you wanted to get high?"

"I don't know, it's not like I really *wanted* to get high," I claimed.

"Well, I went to get beer and I came back and you were down there smoking a fucking doob with some other guy."

"Linda arranged it. I didn't even know what was going on."

"I don't understand. If you wanted to get high you should have just said so instead of hooking up with some douche-bag at a concert," he shouted.

I cried into the window.

"I thought you weren't into that anyway. Since when do you even want to smoke?" he questioned.

"I don't know. We were drinking and laughing and everyone was talking about how they got dime bags and the marijuana…"

"It's called pot, Leigh. Pot."

"Well, everyone made it sound fun and everyone has done it but me." I cried more.

"Still. If you wanted to get high you should have told me instead of letting Linda hook you up with some asshole you don't even know. If you want to get high, I'll get you high," he said.

"What? Where?" I inquired through my tears.

"If you're serious, I'll get you high," he very easily held.

"No… you guys made it sound fun. That wasn't fun at all. That was a horrible experience," I sniffled.

After a long period of silence, Dan said, "Why the fuck were you in the bushes?"

"I was so ashamed of myself. I must've had a bad trip or hit," I guessed.

"Don't do that. You don't even know what you're talking about. You were *drunk*, not stoned." He shook is head at me in disgust.

After that, I managed to stay drug-free for nearly another 15 years. OK, it wasn't that hard. I never had any desire to smoke pot again and I accused people who did hit the pipe of being losers and addicts. In my opinion, they were immature, lazy and couldn't appreciate the value of a good beer buzz. During the FBI application process I rightfully checked "no" next to the "Have you done drugs?" question, but only because it also said "within the last 5 years." Phew! Still, I hoped I wouldn't be asked about that dark phase of my life during the lie detector exam.

As I approached 40, though, the FBI dream slowly became a distant memory. Like a sexy car driving off into the sunset over a long, winding road, I saw it disappear over the horizon with no hope of turning around. Each birthday was a somber reminder that I wasn't that sexy car speeding over the bureaucratic crest. I had too much mileage, my paint was dull, even rusty in some places, and I had a big crack in my back bumper. My fortieth birthday was no different. I awoke with the same apprehensive excitement I did each year — thankful for my many blessings, yet disappointed about the exhilarating life I would never live as a Special Agent. Dan surprised me with a party of our closest friends, at which my friend Rob wrote a song about my infectious personality, perpetual flashing of the boobs, and love of wine.

After much wine consumption, one of the party stragglers suggested getting high.

"FUCK IT!" I said. "I'm ready. I'll do it." I glanced at Dan and he just shook his head.

My dealer friend exited my home and returned shortly thereafter with several items: a lighter, a glass smoking devise that looked like a small penis or glass-blown hummingbird feeder and some weed.

"LET'S DO THIS!" There were a lot more items than just the blunt I threw on the ground at the Allman Brothers concert, though, and I was a little intimidated. *Does this require some sort of assembly? This looks like a science project. Where is my tri-fold poster board?*

"Are you sure you want to do this, Leigh?" my friend asked.

"Yeah. I'm forty years old. The FBI is never going to hire me. I'm ready to get high. It's my fortieth birthday!"

"Alright."

My friend put some stuff that looked like basil or oregano into the pipe, held it up to my lips, lit the spices and calmly directed me to inhale. I inhaled the smoke, held my breath and looked around. I wasn't quite sure what to do once it was in my lungs. I wondered if I could blow circles or fancy smoke shapes, but I didn't want to overdo it on my first try. Then I began to ponder how incredibly stupid it felt to be sitting on my back porch in 40-degree weather smoking pot from a hummingbird feeder. I didn't feel anything. I didn't feel high at all. I didn't feel like one of the cool kids. I felt almost betrayed. Everyone talked about how fun it would be and I just sat there in my un-fun state. I kept asking, "Now what?" to which everyone replied, "That's it." I imagined that my marijuana buzz would hit me like a good liquor buzz. After a few liquor drinks, I know when I'm buzzed. I get a little loud and obnoxious and everything becomes slightly funnier. After smoking marijuana, I sat anxiously waiting for something to happen. My eyes were big as saucers scanning the room waiting for something, anything, to happen.

"Mine didn't work," I pouted.

"Just relax," they said.

Twenty minutes later I stood up, stripped all my clothes off and giggled, "Who wants to go skinny dipping?" That wasn't the weed talking, though — spontaneous stripping wasn't out of the ordinary when I was liquored up.

No one joined me, but my faithful friend Stacey supervised me to make sure I didn't drown. I floated around the pool alone, alternating between the breaststroke and sinking. Once I realized how cold it was outside, I emerged to very adamantly declare that I fancied nachos. I marched into the kitchen and made a respectable platter of nachos and then consumed them in an effort to suppress my feelings of disappointment that I still hadn't gotten high. I surveyed the room, deduced that nothing else exciting was going to happen and announced, "Thank you for coming to my birthday party. I'm going to bed."

It was two more years before I truly completed the long-awaited rite of passage I'd missed out on in my youth and felt the effects of marijuana. I was on vacation when my friend, Sam, casually asked, "Do you want to smoke?" Out of habit, my thoughts immediately turned to the FBI. I'd already had a week that was particularly full of self-doubt, and I was really looking forward to cutting loose on vacation.

With the reminder of the FBI's rejection added to my need to just let go and relax, I conceded, "Sure. Why not?" And just like that, the hummingbird feeder was in my mouth again. I took three big hits; I didn't think it really "took" last time, and I wanted to be sure I actually got high this time. Then Sam and I erected a tent in the back yard and sat down in a couple of beach chairs to admire our handiwork.

I started with the questions. "Now what?"

"Nothing. That's it. Just relax," Sam said.

"I don't feel anything," I maintained.

"You're probably high," he assured me.

"I don't feel high. What am I supposed to feel like?" I asked.

"You might feel like relaxing, listening to music… putting up a tent," he laughed.

"I feel anxious," I mumbled.

"Yeah, you might feel anxious."

"I feel like someone might pop out of the bushes," I said as my eyes darted around the backyard.

He laughed.

"Seriously, I feel really anxious, like I'm waiting for something to happen. Like someone's either going to jump out of the bushes or just go running by streaking," I said.

"Yeah. You're high," he confirmed.

"No, really. I keep waiting for someone to jump out at me. I keep picturing Ed McMahon walking around the corner with a balloon and huge check," I said earnestly.

Sam laughed.

I think my hand is glued to my cup. I can't move my fingers. I feel like I'm melting into my beach chair. Wow, it's really pretty today. This is the prettiest day I have ever seen. The clouds look soft. My hand feels stuck to my cup. Those bushes are green. And big. If someone jumps out of the bushes I hope I don't spill my drink. I wonder if they'll be naked and just run right past me or if they'll stop and flash me. My lip is tingly. I'm thirsty. I wonder if Ed McMahon will know to come around to the backyard to find me.

Sam and I walked inside to refill our drinks.

"We were just organizing the garage," I announced, winking at Sam. No one even acknowledged me. I refilled my cocktail and announced again, "I'm just going to go finish organizing the garage."

We settled into our beach chairs again and Sam said, "So, how was that?"

"OH. MY. GOD. I think they knew," I giggled. "Dude, our tent looks fucking awesome."

"Mmmmm hmmm," Sam agreed. For a while we just sat and stared at the tent in the middle of the backyard while listening to Led Zeppelin.

I surveyed the bushes for the streaker. "So when can we smoke again?" I asked Sam.

"It's 8 o'clock in the morning. Why don't you wait 'til after lunch," he smiled.

"Das cool bro," I nodded my head while gazing into the vacant tent.

I smoked the bud one more time that afternoon before it really hit me. The Cannabis swirled around in my body, mixing with my own dopamine, which triggered a strange curiosity. I felt relaxed, yet invincible. Inquisitive and philosophical. I wondered, if I could be any animal, what animal would I most like to be? I supposed a turtle would be cool. Turtles are so chill. They don't hurt anyone. They're just like, "Hey man, I want to swim, and maybe eat some lettuce. But I'm gonna take my time getting there. I'm not in a rush. Because I'm a turtle."

Suddenly I needed to know how shampoo and conditioner could be effectively combined. And just as abruptly and urgently that inquiry had entered my mind, it was gone and I realized that Goldfish crackers were always smiling. Was it because they were baked, like me? My mind was mimicking Newton's Cradle with increased momentum and energy slamming random thoughts into one another. Why had no one invented a clear toaster so you can see how toasted your bread is getting while it's toasting? Were oranges the only fruit pre-sliced by nature? If I owned a funeral home, I could get a parrot and teach it to say, "Help! They've turned me into a parrot!" That would be epic. *Yes, that's it*, I settled. *I should buy a parrot and a funeral home.*

I lost all sense of time, just being stoned and marveling at life beyond my beach chair. I wondered how many missed connections I had had in life. Had Dan and I ever crossed paths before we met? Were there people I had yet to befriend who I'd already passed on the street? In other cities, even? Where did this weed come from? Had I ever passed the dealer on the street? I contemplated where Felicity's future husband might be *right then*? Did he live in our city? What could he be doing? Was his mother cool? Was she getting high?

I was suddenly aware of *finally* being high, and enjoyed the feeling. Then I spent some time painstakingly speculating whether or not there was a way to bury a car with a sunroof in the ground so you could climb down through the sunroof to get baked and chill out underground.

Although my mind battled to keep up with the thoughts knocking around in head, my body was calm and undisturbed. I carefully studied how my boobs just rested atop my chest, unrestricted in simply a swimsuit. *Interesting.* I never noticed how bouncy and squishy breasts were until I realized I'd been holding my boob for five minutes. It was like a warm stress-relieving ball. *I guess guys aren't morons, after all,* I reflected, and finally understood why men love titties. Once my mind finally slowed to my body's physical stillness, I fell into a four-hour slumber while drooling and cupping my left boob.

That was the last time I partied with Mary J. I was awake that entire night, hallucinating that all my teeth were falling out of my head. It was a trip — and not a trip I want to take again. I'm happy to stick to my liquor buzz; it goes better with my Milli Vanilli tunes anyway.

Ten

Postpartum Depression: The Gift That Keeps on Giving

I carefully slithered onto the couch, my face squinted in pain as I held my breath. Using excruciating care, I hiked one partially-numb leg onto a stack of chenille throw pillows, left the other leg dangling toward the floor, placed a bag of frozen corn on my sore vagina, let out an earthy sigh, and sank deep into the sofa. "Ahhh..."

"We're at war! We're at war!" my mother screamed.

It sounded overly dramatic, like the way you scream when your child locks himself in a department store dressing room and you have to find a clerk to let him out. Do you abandon your child and personal belongings as you frantically run to the front of the store in search of help, or do you stand your post, screaming for the jaws-of-life to free your sweet Billy from the dressing room? Either way, you look like a lunatic, which is exactly what my mother looked like as she frantically shrieked, "We're at war! We're at war!"

My mother has a tendency to exaggerate. But this time, she was right. We *were* at war.

My mom was in town to help out, because just three blissful days earlier Dan and I were in the hospital having our first baby. Well, *we* weren't having a baby — *I* was having the baby. I'm the one with the vagina, so technically it was just me *having* the baby. I hate when couples say, "We're pregnant!" or "We're having a baby!" I just want to respond, "No you're not. You have a dick, and only the one with a uterus can have the baby."

I had always dreamed of the day I'd bring my baby home from the hospital. I could just see myself strolling into the foyer in my size 4 Lucky Brand jeans and white J. Crew tank top, pink balloons jostling around me merrily while I carried the next blue-eyed, blonde-haired Drew Barrymore-esque child star into her new home. Although we lived in Del Mar, I was absolutely certain my baby would be spotted at the local market by some big-shot director who was passing through town on the way to his beachfront cottage in La Jolla. After all, isn't that where all the biggest stars are discovered — in the grocery store?

All I ever wanted to be in life was a mother. Well, what I *really* wanted to be was a Special Agent in the Federal Bureau of Investigations, but before I discovered the allure of becoming an FBI Agent (and then again after the FBI decided they didn't want me) I had dreams of becoming a mother. I grew up babysitting my neighbor's four boys, so from the time I was 11 years old I wanted to be a mother to a litter of boys. That is, until I got pregnant; then I suddenly wanted a girl.

I remember the day Dan and I started trying to have a baby. It was three months after our honeymoon and we decided we were ready.

No one is ready for a baby, by the way. No one tells you the bad shit. No one tells you that you'll never sleep again. No one tells you that this devil child will make you homicidal. No one tells you about the mustard-colored poop, the projectile vomit, taking its temperature up the ass, wearing the same clothes for four days straight, not showering for weeks on end, constantly smelling like vomit and feces, the amount of laundry, the price of Stride Rite shoes. (For God's sake, why are baby shoes so expensive? They can't even walk! The soles of their shoes could just as easily be sewn from soft tortillas.) But there's a cult of parents out there who won't tell you these things. You tell them you're pregnant and they're like, "Congratulations!" while secretly thinking, "You're so fucked. You don't even *know* how fucked you are."

Of course we knew it wouldn't be easy, but Dan and I thought we were better than most people and that our collective superiority would make us better parents than everyone else. *We are college-educated adults. Surely, we have nothing to worry about.* We read every parenting book and boldly declared our parenting style, which did not include the family bed or spanking of any kind. We renewed our subscription to Consumer Reports to research every baby product known to mankind, and only elected to register for items with a 4.5 star rating or higher. But while people gave us kind advice like "breast is best," not one of those motherfuckers told us about the bad shit. It was like they were giggling to themselves inside — a screeching, evil, haunted house giggle. They knew they had converted one more couple to parenthood. Two more fools had crossed the line and come over to the dark side.

Nevertheless, we dove in headfirst and made a baby. Figuratively, of course; going in headfirst doesn't make babies. See? I know more about oral sex now.

I had an uneventful pregnancy, unless you count the three times I went to the Scripps Hospital for false labor pains. Who knew a fetus could have the hiccups? I enjoyed nearly every moment of being pregnant: the glow, the tubs of ice cream, the voluptuous breasts. *Ohhhh*, the breasts. They were a welcome addition to the prepubescent boy body I was used to. I embraced their existence and flaunted them like a cheap whore.

I purchased sheer, lacy bras that my flat frame hadn't previously allowed me the luxury of filling, along with equally transparent, low-cut blouses. I would often drop by Dan's office unexpectedly in my translucent ensemble to show off my plump breasts and entice him to touch them in the lobby. "Put some fucking clothes on," he'd bark at me. When he'd arrive home from work I would often be sprawled out on the couch with my developing breasts exposed, demanding that he fondle them. "Suck on my titties," I would order him like a drill sergeant. From the chest up I was a sultry vixen wanting him to caress my newly ample bosom; from the midline down I was a round, waddling duck in elastic cargo sweatpants from Old Navy.

I especially enjoyed eating for two, and took every opportunity to consume extra calories — you know, *for the baby.* My snack of choice was Ding Dongs. And burritos. Big, fat burritos with extra guacamole and black bean salsa. I single-handedly kept the Del Mar Baja Fresh in business for those nine months. I added 68 pounds to my tiny frame and proudly wobbled around, flaunting my girth and swollen breasts. My obstetrician didn't seem concerned with my excess weight gain either, and never warned me that I was getting dangerously close to delivering a small elephant. He'd say the same things at each appointment. "Wow! Another 26 pounds," or "Hmm… that scale isn't working today, let's get you out back to the loading dock," or "You know the drill: undress from the waist down and drape this circus tent around your fat ass."

I read all the parenting books, decorated the nursery according to the U.S. Consumer Product Safety Commission website — no lead paint products, no hanging cords on the mini-blinds, crib facing exactly northwest away from the window just in case "the big one" hit California — and took the appropriate birthing and La Leche classes. My birthing plan was rather flexible, with the only firm requirement being that if I needed an episiotomy I didn't want to *hear* the cut of my taint; I strictly directed my doctor that if he needed to cut me, he should cough, sneeze or throw the surgical utensils across the room to trigger a loud distraction. With all those particulars planned, I was sufficiently prepared and well on my way to being the *perfect* mother.

Until September 11th, 2001.

While I bought time between contractions with focused breathing, someone else was focused on buying a plane ticket. I was nervous, yet they were eerily calm. As I threw up the last thing I ate, they knowingly ate their last meal. While I pushed new life I cared about so deeply into the world, they carelessly packed their belongings into their luggage. While my new family drove out of the hospital parking lot, they were driving to the airport. Then, after I walked into our new home and introduced our sweet baby to her flawless world, they deliberately flew airplanes into buildings and introduced true horror to that world.

That's when my life and plans to be the perfect mother were turned upside down.

Our first night home from the hospital was torment. Our tiny angel, Felicity, cried nearly non-stop. Her arms and legs flailed around like an epileptic and her face turned red as fire. She was pissed off. She hated me, my swollen breasts and everything I had to offer. According to Mr. Webster and his big book of fancy words, "felicity" meant happiness. This wasn't happiness; this was hell.

I spent nearly an hour coaxing her to latch onto my engorged breast. I tweaked and twisted my nipple between my thumb and forefinger to drip just enough breast milk onto her lips; the scent was supposed to make her instinctively latch on, but she looked like a blind person with her limbs tied behind her back bobbing for apples. She got increasingly agitated as her head whipped back and forth. With each bob, I would try again to thrust my boob against her mouth. Once she *finally* latched on, I sank into the rocking chair feeling victorious and defeated all in the same breath.

She suckled for six whole minutes before the bout started again. I grabbed my log, dutifully wrote down "six minutes" under the Left Breast heading and switched my bracelet to the right wrist. My left breast, a hefty C-cup, felt deflated in comparison to the engorged right breast. And the dance began again. She bobbed. I thrusted. She bobbed. I cried. She seized and flailed. I thrusted and sobbed. Again, she finally latched on and I sank into the rocker feeling beaten yet proud. This time she suckled for 18 minutes before pulling away from my breast. Her eyes were glazed over with drunken fullness. The corner of her lips curled up slightly to one side as my milk dribbled back out onto my chest. I curled her into my tired hands, hoisted her onto my shoulder and patted gently.

"BrrRRRrrrrrrrPPPPppppppp!"

Fluid spewed from her lips, over my shoulder and across the room, slamming into the wall behind the rocking chair with surprising force. She gasped for air as a frothy fluid filled her lungs, contracted and then shot out at warp speed. The room, which had finally been graced with sweet silence just moments before, was again filled with a high-pitched cry, aggravating enough to make you voluntarily plunge a sharp, rusty object into your own eye socket.

"Oh my God! Go get my mom!" I yelled to Dan.

"Suzy! It's puking!" Dan screamed down the hallway.

My mother, a nurse, swaddled and comforted Felicity while I paced the floor and Dan looked for the phone.

"Mom, what do I do?" I pleaded.

"She probably got a little too much to eat and just spit up," my mother said calmly.

"But she, like, puked a ton," I panted.

My mom rocked Felicity gently to sleep as I cried on the floor. Thoughts swirled around in my mind weightlessly like sugar in a cotton candy machine, sweet and toxic thoughts weaving around one another, bound together with implausibility. I thought, "Do I put her to bed on an empty stomach? What if she starves to death her first hour home? Do I feed her again? This wasn't in *What to Expect When You're Expecting*. What if she was born without a stomach?"

This was a genuine, certifiable emergency. Dan knew it and handed me the phone.

"9-1-1. What's your emergency?"

Yes? Hi! I just had a baby and I packed my skinny jeans into my cute little hospital duffel bag hoping to wear them home today, but they don't fit. And I'm too embarrassed to wear the size XL sweatpants with the broken elastic in the waist and hole in the crotch that came from my legs rubbing together while I was pregnant. I don't want those pants featured in the first-day-home photos of me with my beautiful baby that get hot glued into the scrap book of her first 24 hours at home with me... because when she gets married she'll be so embarrassed that her mother had on ugly, torn maternity sweatpants instead of a cute Japanese Weekend shrug in our first photo op...

"Hello? 9-1-1. What's your emergency?"

"Oh! I'm sorry. Hello? My baby just projectile vomited more than her body weight onto the wall. What should I do?"

"Ma'am, is your baby breathing?" the operator calmly asked.

Before or after I put the pillow over her head?

"Yes, I believe so."

"OK. Are you certain that the baby is breathing?" she needed to confirm.

"Yes," I finally established.

"What you need to do, ma'am, is call your pediatrician's after-hours line and they will help you," she advised.

"OK. I'll do that RIGHT NOW!"

"Triage. Can I help you?" asked the pediatric nurse.

"Yes. My baby just puked everywhere," I declared, as if that would clarify everything.

"OK. And who is your baby?" she asked.

"The one who was crying with her head still in my vagina and Dr. Lee said, 'Wow, in all my years delivering babies, I've never seen a baby cry *before* they came out of the birth canal.' That one."

"OK. Does the baby have a temperature?"

"I don't know."

"OK. I will need you to take the baby's temperature," she instructed.

"Umm… OK…"

"Do you have a thermometer?"

"I don't know. Dan, go look through the baby gifts and see if someone gave us a thermometer."

(several minutes later…)

"OK. We have a thermometer!" I said victoriously.

"OK. Good. I will need you to take the baby's temperature."

"Well, now she's asleep," I said, perplexed by the situation.

"OK. We still need to know if she has a temperature," she nudged.

"OK."

"You can just lubricate the thermometer and take a rectal reading."

"A what?"

"A rectal reading. Just lubricate the thermometer really good," she assured me.

"Lubricate it with what?" I was dumbfounded.

"Do you have any Vaseline?"

"I don't know. Dan, go see if we have any Vaseline." *(several minutes later…)*

"We don't have any Vaseline," I said.

"OK. You can use olive oil or vegetable oil," she said.

"From the kitchen?" *That's gross.*

"Yes. Anything to lubricate it would be fine."

"Dan, go see if we have any olive oil or vegetable oil."

(several more minutes of awkward silence on the phone…)

"We don't have any oil. Look, we just had our first baby and ate out every night before today. We don't cook or have vegetable oil in our house," I said, defeated.

"You can use butter," she suggested.

"Butter? I'm not sticking butter in my baby's butt."

"It's important that we know if she has a temperature," she insisted.

"Hold on…"

(another few minutes…)

"How's Astroglide?" I mumbled into the phone away from my mother's ears.

"Perfect," the triage nurse said, the first sign of exhaustion evident in her voice.

"OK. I need to put the phone down."

"That's fine. Take your time."

"Dan, put her on the changing table… try not to wake her up. I can't get these snaps undone... the buttons go up the back... her foot is stuck… OK… you hold her feet… never mind, hold her face down… and I'll stick the thingy in... DAN! HOLD HER!"

"THE THING WON'T STAY IN," he yelled at me.

"THEN CLINCH HER ASS CHEEKS TOGETHER," I hollered.

"I CAN'T! YOU CLINCH HER ASS CHEEKS TOGETHER!"

"This isn't working," I said, completely exasperated. "Great! Now she just shit everywhere."

Mustard-yellow feces covered her once-cute outfit, the pink chenille changing pad cover, the newly painted nursery wall and the carpet. Felicity was awake, pissed off and crying at a volume I had not yet heard. I started to cry. I wanted earplugs. I wanted a beer. I wanted to shove this baby back into my vagina. "Where's that Astroglide?" I said. "Just shove her back in my pussy! If I could just get one more day of sleep, I'm sure I'd be more prepared for this tomorrow."

After we determined she did not have a temperature and the situation was not 9-1-1 worthy, my mother swaddled the baby tightly and calmed her down while Dan and I paced. I frantically flipped through all my parenting books to see if I should feed her again or if she might, in fact, starve to death within hours of coming home from the hospital. My mother retrieved a medicine dropper from the kitchen and gave Felicity one dropper full of water to moisten her lips and, presumably, rinse the residual vomit out of the mouth.

"What are you doing?" I screamed at my mother.

"Just giving her a little water," my mother defended herself.

"You can't give her water. No one said that was OK. That's not in the books!"

"Leigh, it's just water," my mom said.

"I'm only supposed to give her breast milk. What if she's allergic to water or chokes on it?" I cried. "Or worse, what if she dies?"

"From water?" my mom inquired with a concerned look on her face.

"You don't know! You don't know what you're doing!"

"Well, I raised two children myself and have been a nurse for over 30 years," she calmly assured me. "One drop of water will be OK."

"Give me my baby!" I shrieked as I snatched her out of my mother's grip.

I spent all night coaxing Felicity into short, sporadic moments of slumber; when the sun finally shone through the window, I vanquished any notion that I would get any rest that night. I wearily gathered the baby and re-located downstairs on the couch, in the same clothes I had been wearing since I was admitted into the hospital, hoping for any comfort or normalcy.

Within minutes my mother was screaming, "We're at war! We're at war!"

Dan came running downstairs, trying to process what that could have meant. Had Felicity thrown up again, or shit all over another wall? My mother pointed to the television screen, and shock waves went through us all as we listened to what the journalists were suggesting. I held onto my baby with an unparalleled level of fear and desperation as I saw national destruction unfold on the screen. My anxiety and horror seeped from every pore and flooded over Felicity's innocent body. She sensed my terror and became increasingly agitated. Too tired to cry and too scared to breathe, we clung to one another with utter despair. What should have been the most joyous occasion in my life twisted into the beginnings of postpartum depression, which unbeknownst to me would burst into my life with unrelenting cruelty as the days went on.

I positioned a rocking chair smack in front of the television in our bedroom and another one in the family room, where I watched the planes fly into the World Trade Center buildings over and over and over again; I don't remember sleeping that first week of Felicity's life. With each impact of a plane, both Felicity's and my bodies would seize up into knots until we finally surrendered to tears. Nearly every waking moment she cried and, eventually, her tears turned into blood-curdling screams until she was completely inconsolable. Oh, she may have subsided briefly to eat, but she quickly reclaimed her outrage once she was done suckling — gaining deafening momentum with each wail.

Much of the country was closed for business the week of September 11th, including Dan's office. Since he couldn't go to work or soothe Felicity any more than I could, he thought a simple trip to Home Depot would prove worthwhile — both for his productivity and sanity. However, the mere mention of him leaving me alone with the baby to go out into the unpredictable and dangerous world sent me into a tailspin that I had not anticipated. Our future and safety felt uncertain, and I speculated wildly about a plane or something much worse targeting us. I was certain the Home Depot in San Diego, California was next on Al Qaeda's list of marks. Dan tried to reason with me in my erratic state, but I became increasingly unhinged at the thought of him leaving. I unwittingly found myself lying on the ground, gripping his ankles like a toddler, begging him to stay. He stared at the empty shell of me, unable to recognize the person I had suddenly transformed into. He wasn't the only one who didn't recognize me. I couldn't identify my distorted body, with my sagging gut and bleeding, leaky breasts, and I certainly wasn't familiar with the erratic and fearful thoughts in my mind — *what if I accidentally put the baby in the blender?*

The ambitious and enthusiast girl I knew was quickly fading away. My once confident, driven demeanor gave way to an unrecognizable, shadowy version of myself. Once agile and athletic, I could no longer sneeze without spontaneously peeing my britches. Since giving birth, standing upright felt like my guts were floating around inside my body and each trip to the bathroom produced blood clots the size of tennis balls, requiring me to wear hospital-issued gauze diapers that were a far cry from the sheer, lacy bras I'd felt so sexy in mere weeks earlier. And those same motherfuckers who didn't warn me about parenthood also neglected to caution me about hemorrhoids. My formerly taut little ass now had what felt like a vine of grapes dangling from between my flaccid cheeks. Too embarrassed to discuss it with my doctor, I kept them clean and quietly tucked them back into my asshole. The voluptuous breasts I grew so fond of became more utilitarian than decorative and sexually gratifying. Hearing *any* baby (or feral cat) cry caused me to spring a leak worthy of taking down a small fishing vessel. I cared less about my appearance than Kirstie Alley in her heavy days and fashioned complete outfits from bed sheets and burp cloths.

Worse than my pitiful appearance was my despondent mindset, which slowly diminished my ability to function. I was sleep-deprived and developed widespread fears about Felicity's safety — what if she stopped breathing or choked? I prematurely performed the Heimlich maneuver at the first sign of any audible distress, which was often and could account for her now slightly askew spine, and concluded that no one was qualified to hold her except me. I was too distraught and disorganized to leave the house, so I sat alone and cried most days. On one memorable occasion I tried to venture out, but Felicity had some sort of hypersensitive reaction to being put in a car seat. She cried so severely that she turned purple and I had to pull off the road; I paced with her in the breakdown lane until Dan picked us up and nervously escorted us back home. I backed myself into a corner there, where I felt trapped by my own ridiculous constraints and felt more and more isolated and depressed.

While Dan grew somewhat accustomed to my unrealistic fears and constant tearful outbursts, he remained vigilant in watching for more concerning behavior. When Felicity was just six weeks, old he came home from work one morning to check on me, which he often did, and found Felicity red-faced and crying in her bouncy seat just steps outside of the shower. It was hardly 10:00 in the morning and I was sitting on the floor of the blistering shower drinking an ice-cold beer. For breakfast. I was overwhelmed with feelings of failure, exhaustion and absolute hopelessness. Dan took me to my OBGYN, and he recommended that I consider taking "a little something to take the edge off." I don't know why I was surprised — I had been labeled crazy before — but this time it felt much crueler. It felt like someone was saying to me that in order for me to be a good mother, I had to be medicated; that I couldn't be good at it *naturally*. It wasn't that I wanted to suffocate my baby or send her up a stream swaddled in a cashmere blanket. I didn't want to hurt her at all; in fact, I didn't want her out of my sight.

What I wanted, however, was to sleep longer than the dishwasher cycle and to sit Felicity down long enough to take a shit without inducing a full-blown grand mal seizure (in either of us). I wanted to shave *both* legs in the shower instead of jumping out early because I couldn't stand the sound her screams penetrating the bathroom door. I wanted to eat a warm meal at the dining room table with my husband, instead of a piece of pie someone gifted us while I sat in a rocking chair upstairs feeling detached and desperately trying to rock Felicity to sleep. I wanted, just once, to not have to call Dan at work and ask him to get takeout yet again because I was drowning in my own tears and couldn't construct some sort of dinner other than leftover pie. I wanted to sleep in my own bed instead of on the floor alongside Felicity's crib, plotting the perfect moment to crawl out of her room without waking her up.

I held onto that medicine for a few weeks, questioning what to do and wondering how many similar prescriptions were given to other new mothers the week of September 11th. What I knew for sure was that Felicity deserved better than what she was getting from me at that moment. It wasn't her fault our country had been attacked, and if I needed "a little something to take the edge off" while we sorted out all the domestic implications, then so be it.

Once I embraced the medicine, I was finally able to relax; the unrealistic fears dissipated and the endless anxiety gradually melted away. Felicity grew less colicky, her delightful personality emerged and we began to enjoy each other's company. I began to relish motherhood and everything it had to offer — surprises and all — and celebrate the nominal milestones. Big and little events tested my perseverance; our first earthquake was not at all as catastrophic as I predicted, but merely a highlight on her baby calendar.

Then our first excursion out of the house happened, and it proved to be even less disastrous and more laughable than I first expected. It was a beautiful afternoon and I was tired of feeling confined to the house, so I pulled on something without elastic for the first time in almost a year and ventured out for a girls' shopping trip. Felicity and I landed at Pier 1 Imports for our first stop. After tootling around briefly, I thought it best to refashion the backpack-style diaper bag that had been dangling off one shoulder. I gazed around, considered any possible threats or choking hazards, sat Felicity on the tile floor and *quickly* positioned the additional strap over my second shoulder. In that split-second, Felicity snatched something up and heaved it into her mouth. I instantly flipped her upside down, pounded on her back and performed the "J" hook finger sweep inside her mouth — but nothing materialized. I was so distraught that terror crept in again within a nanosecond; I began to cry and immediately drove back home to our safe haven. The following afternoon Felicity took a shit in her diaper, which up until then had been a mustard-tinged pancake batter consistency. This time it was a solid brown, sausage-like log and, upon closer inspection, there was a shiny gold sticker perfectly affixed to the outside of her turd that read *Made in China.*

At that precise moment I recognized that motherhood was going to require, along with a CPR certification and a little medicine, an inordinate amount of patience and a sense of humor. Just when I thought I couldn't bear it any longer, something amusing typically happened — a soggy Cheerio sneezed from a nostril, a Houdini-like escape from secured pajamas or a giggle-induced sudsy flatulence attack in the bathtub — and the best one of all, the *Made in China* piece of shit. Each colossal defeat led to an even greater pleasure and reward; every tear book-ended by a smile or a happy coo. Eventually the tearful days faded away and boisterous giggles washed away the memories of failure and hopelessness.

Confidence and cheerful optimism seeped back into our lives and I became pregnant with our second baby. And those same motherfuckers who neglected to warn me of rectal temperatures, hemorrhoids and postpartum depression, never once let it slip that twice the children does not equal twice the amount of work. One plus one does not equal two.

Trying to quantify the exponential increase in workload with the negative exponent of sleep is like, well solving Fermat's Last Theorem. It took over 358 years of effort by the most respected mathematicians to solve that theory, but somehow the sum of one child plus one more is a much more difficult quandary to solve.

I did the math on this one and it looks something like this:

$$1 + 1 = 3(-sleep) + \frac{wine}{antidepressant} + 1 + laundry^2 \frac{sanity}{personal\ hygiene} = dinner$$

Solve for dinner.

Answer: π *is for dinner.*

Eleven

AND GIVING

*C*ameron was right side up — well, upside down in the gynecological world — hence *breached*. But because I had a scheduled C-section, I was less concerned about my tender taint and more anxious about introducing Felicity to the heir to her potty throne. I had read enough parenting books to know that if we doted all over "the baby" it was likely that we would find "the baby" duct taped to the bottom of the swimming pool with horribly-arched eyebrows Sharpied onto his bloated face. Therefore, my single wish when Cameron was born was that Dan and I quietly and lovingly introduce Felicity to her little brother. Alone. My desire was to gently and very prudently welcome Cameron into our family, all while diverting the excitement and attention away from "the baby" and solely onto Felicity becoming a big sister. Yay!

I should have known better. If I had learned one thing in my short time as a mother, it was to avoid making rigid plans. Well, making any plans at all with children is somewhat futile, but especially making proposals so inflexible that an entire sibling relationship is hinged on, let's say, the wattage of the light bulb at your perfectly imagined introduction. And, perhaps more importantly, to lower your expectations when said plans fall apart. Like, really low. Lower.

Once the cesarean surgery was over, I was transported down a long, brightly lit hallway to a recovery room with Dan trailing closely behind my bed, rolling Cameron in his hospital-appointed bassinet. As we continued down the corridor, we passed an elevator carriage where I heard a *ding!* followed by surprising commotion and jostled excitement. Before I realized what was happening, Dan's parents and Felicity intercepted Dan, the bassinet and its contents in the noisy hallway where they introduced Felicity to "the baby" for the first time, under the bright fluorescent lights among the hustle and bustle of the Labor and Delivery floor with cooing, impatient grandparents orchestrating the entire introduction.

The surgical nurse continued to roll me down the lively hallway. I heard vague, faint squeals whilst we rounded the corner into my recovery room. Numb from anesthesia, I wasn't even able to crane my neck around to see the distant expression on Felicity's face as she met "the baby." Perhaps she was envisioning how high to arch the eyebrows? I'll never know; I missed that tender moment and, just like when Felicity was born, my plan to be the perfect mother was shattered. For one desolate moment I sat alone in my room and cried. I wept out of fear. Fear that someone else was orchestrating what I thought to be the one thing I had control over – *how* I nurtured my children. And just like Felicity, I had no control over my child's first moments in this world; the realization that I couldn't care for and protect them the way I planned crushed me with a paralyzing force. This child, whom I once solely confined and guarded, was now outside of my body at the mercy of an incompetent and unloving world. I struggled to combat the suffocating feelings entering my mind and tried to claw my way to the surface to breathe. No matter the effort, I felt robbed, inadequate, incapable and hopeless all over again.

Our first night home with Cameron met us with the same anxiety-inducing, bloodcurdling cries we were greeted by with Felicity on 9/11. Cameron, who was also colicky, cried with the same steady urgency Felicity had. When I closed my eyes, it was like nothing had changed since those awful first days home with Felicity and I felt anxious, tired and scared.

However, instead of a torn, cavernous hole that formed one single vagina-butthole, I now had a gaping wound in my abdomen being held together with office supplies. The cesarean slash was raw, oozing in some parts and threatening to explode open like a gory Subway sandwich commercial. I could hardly maneuver around the house, let alone heave myself into our towering four-poster bed; even without a belly wound I needed a stepladder to carefully climb into our lofty bed. Post-op, as I prudently ascended the steps, I felt my innermost guts wiggle and jiggle inside me, causing me pause. It was during my suspension on the top wooden stair, as I tried to catch my breath amidst the searing pain in my stomach, when BAM! BOOM! CRASH! The top stair gave way and I sliced through the lower three steps, sending splintering pieces of pine every direction and my fat ass straight to the floor. I let out a wail loud enough to challenge any sizable earthquake, clutched my tummy and began to cry. Dan rushed to my side, not knowing if I was simply shaken or if my appendix and large intestine were suddenly tangled in the woody bed skirt. Once he determined that I was purely emotionally scarred from having my big butt smash through an entire step ladder, he assembled a twin size trundle bed a mere six inches off the floor in the corner of our bedroom for me to sleep on during my six-week post-cesarean recovery.

Aside from the physical discomfort, emotionally I felt like there was a sniper tracking me at all times. Depression is the highly trained, often not lethal but dangerous nonetheless, sniper who maintains constant visual contact with its target (new mom) from concealed positions or from distances exceeding detection capabilities of enemy personnel (family and friends). And while snipers typically operate alone, Postpartum Depression is a sophisticated marksman, working with a combat team of Hopelessness, Anxiety and Weepiness. Postpartum is a sharpshooter extremely well trained in camouflage, field craft, infiltration, special reconnaissance and observation, surveillance and target acquisition. Each moment when I felt optimistic and thought *this time will be different*, he lodged a bullet of disbelief in me. For every small gain — an early bath (ready, aim); a sizable setback — an explosive diaper requiring an expansive carpet shampoo (fire!). For each emotional triumph — feeling hopeful, even cheerful, about the day (ready, aim); an even bigger barricade — an unexplained, excessive fever landing us in the E.R. all night (fire!). Once again, I was in the cross hairs of depression feeling drained, hopeless, and incompetent on the grandest scale (target hit). No amount of camouflage could conceal me from the explosives being shot at me. Exhausted (pthew!), delirious (pthew!), worried (pthew!), despondent (pthew!), insecure, unsafe and desperate (pthew-pthew-pthew!).

And just like that I was lying on the neglected, mildewed tile of the blistering shower having beer for breakfast again.

Call in the Extraction Team!

Hello, Lexapro and Wellbutrin. It's nice to see you again. And, what the fuck took you so long?

The pills went down a little easier the second time around.

Several months later, I waltzed into my local Starbucks with Felicity toddling about in her adorable summer ensemble; Cameron was also dressed, wiped clean and securely mounted on my hip. I happily placed my coffee order feeling rather proud that I managed to get us clothed and out of the house before sundown with minimal crying spells — primarily by me.

The crunchy barista looked up from her java-stained, Kelly green apron, readied her black marker and said, "Aww, your kids are soooo cute," then studied me briskly and added, "They must look just like their dad."

Excuse me?

What the fuck am I?

Dog meat?

I was dressed too. Also clean. Presentable. I like to think of myself as average to slightly above average, if

I'm being honest, in terms of beauty and probably even a little higher where hygiene is concerned. I'm not a three-legged hunchback with a third eyeball peering out of my forehead. No chin hairs, yet, or unsightly moles on the tip of my nose. I wasn't disheveled and drooling into my hoodie like at the airport Starbucks. How dare she insult me! Maybe Dan was the ugly one. Perhaps our beautiful children got their stunning good looks from *me*. I wanted to say, "Actually, my husband was born without ears, has one leg eight inches longer than the other, horribly dry hair and elephantiasis of the balls." She didn't know.

It was moments like that — when I felt joyful, satisfied, and secure in my mothering — when something or someone could unexpectedly take the wind out of my sails... then tip my boat upside down and tie an anchor to it. Just when I thought I was going to make it through postpartum, doubt — dreadful, all-consuming doubt — inexplicably crept back in and told me I wasn't a good mother or homemaker or wife. Simple words and moments weighed heavily on me while other mothers seemed to brush them off, go with the flow. People describe certain idiosyncrasies, like open-mouth chewing or knuckle cracking, comparable to *nails on a chalkboard*. Just sends them over the edge, they say. For me, it was other things. Everything actually.

Like Getting In and Out of the Car

Every single time we approached the car, the kids would stand precisely smack dab in *front* of the locked door handle, their little bodies and skulls pressed right up against the car door. Every. Single. Fucking. Time. And each time I would shove gently usher them to the side, explaining the door had to open *outward* several feet in order for them to get into the car. Every. Single. Fucking. Time. I wanted to say, "Have you ever seen us enter the car through osmosis? EVER?" Or something a little more forward like, "Have you ever once, just once, seen Mommy ZAP! us into the fucking car? No! Because that's not how we *enter* the car, is it? No. We oooooooppppeeennnnnn the door like this." Or finally, "Get the fuck out of the way!"

The same could be said for the house door or shopping mall door or [insert any place of business] door. Every. Single. Fucking. Time. Their little bodies suctioned to the door like a magnetic plate had inexplicably pulled them to that exact spot right in front of the door. "Excuse me," I would say behind gritted teeth. "I have to *unlock* the ~~fuck-ing~~ door before you can get in. Scooch over, sweetie." And eventually, "Get the fuck out of the way!"

Like Toilet Training

Cameron never liked going to the bathroom. Not in the civilized way, anyhow. The first few weeks of his life he curiously only had a bowel movement when I took a rectal temperature. I, being tired and weary, recognized this early on and rather than wait for his gaseous and distressed belly to produce a stool, would shove a thermometer up his ass to stimulate a bowel movement so that I could hurry us along to bed. The pediatrician scolded me, saying the rectum is a muscle that Cameron needed to learn to strengthen and control himself and not through *artificial stimulation.* I was perfectly willing, however, to follow him to college artificially stimulating his asshole. I was tired. Call it mother's little encouragement.

When he finally did have jurisdiction over his own asshole, he would only shit in a *fresh* diaper. I know what shitting in a fresh diaper leads to — only shitting in the comfort of your own home. I didn't want that kind of life for him. No cross-country road trips or overseas flights, no lengthy mocha-sipping afternoons at Starbucks, no double features at the movies or beachside camping. I wanted him to enjoy the revolutionary achievement of being able to *drop the kids off at the pool* anywhere. There's freedom in prairie-dogging wherever you want, so it really irked me that he required a fresh diaper to drop a deuce. When he finally *did* get comfortable taking a shit in a worn diaper, I couldn't get him to ultimately take the Brown's to the Super Bowl. I vividly recall restraining him to the toilet bowl like a combative inmate, trying to force him to poop in the potty while motioning towards the remote control monster truck box a few feet away.

"If you just poop *in* the potty you can open the box and play with the truck," I bribed while detaining him.

He settled on bashing the unopened box around the slick kitchen floor while comfortably shitting his pants. For six months he shoved that tattered and unopened truck around the house. By the time he finally shat in the toilet, he was uninterested in opening the weathered, dilapidated box housing the monster truck.

Like Accidents

Felicity was more civilized in expelling her bodily waste. She was compliant, eager even, to potty train. Until Cameron was born. Though she had been using the toilet for well over a year, she regressed and began pissing in the floor. Her accidents weren't haphazard middle-of-the-night episodes fostered by too-long days at the park. As a matter of fact, they weren't "accidents" at all. They were calculated, premeditated attempts devised to make me crack. She loitered in the hallway like a fucking cheetah and lay in wait as I nursed Cameron to sleep behind closed doors. And just when I *finally* got him to sleep, she'd pounce through the door with pigtails flopping about and piss on his floor causing me to *shush!* and *shoo!* her — inevitably waking Cameron and yielding great big crocodile tears from him. Then eventually me. Each time, she happily drifted in and out of empty rooms while I nursed Cameron to sleep and then seized the moment by ambushing me like the little predator she was. She'd sweetly look me square in the face with urine running down her leg, knowing I wouldn't lurch out of that rocking chair to jerk the little pony tail off her still-intact-skull.

Like Traveling

While isolation is torturous in its own right, traveling didn't provide any consolation. Packing for any trip with an infant, regardless of duration, was like preparing for Armageddon with the distinct possibility that only the baby would survive. The time and effort spent on packing, labeling and affixing laminated instructions to every article in the rare event an alien spaceship singularly extracts McSweetie in the Apocalypse is all-consuming. Our little cherub needed both the necessities and luxuries to which I'd so foolishly encouraged him to grow accustomed. Stuffed monkey, expensive shoes for tiny immobile feet, four blue-not-purple sippy cups along with a few back-up cups in case the blue ones faded to purple during the earth's explosion, Pooh pacifier clippy thing, Goodnight Moon (large coffee table version because, naturally, he liked that one more than the transportable, pocket-sized variety), sound machine the size of an industrial air conditioning unit to soothe him to sleep, colossal tri-folding cardboard room divider painted in the same hue as his bedroom so he could fall asleep in a familiar setting, same-scent laundry detergent and portable oxygen tanks containing an air sample from his serene nursery. And how can I forget the vomit-stained blue pack-n-play that has never felt the likes of a slumbering head in all its worldly travels; putting Cameron even slightly *near* the playpen caused him to violently puke, although I schlepped it around North America with the hope he would one day suddenly overcome his severe aversion to it.

Basically, I packed the entire contents of our household for him to experience great adventure without the traumatizing realization that he'd left home.

Like Traveling with Husbands

Husbands contribute to postpartum depression in their own *special* way. During those early child-rearing days, Dan typically popped into work early to "just get a few emails out" and returned home at precisely the same moment the taxi pulled into the driveway to pick us up for our vacation. He, more often than not, cheerfully declared, "Let me just throw my stuff in a bag and I'll be ready," with a complete disregard for how, exactly, the children, pets and myself readied ourselves for said vacation. He would inevitably ask, just as the plane taxied down the runway, "Did you pack [insert any random abso-fucking-lutely necessary accouterment either child required]?" To which I responded, "Of course, I did." And again while climbing to 35,000 feet, "Did you board the dog?" Another, "Of course," through gritted teeth. "Did you stop the mail?" *We get mail? At our home? Gasp!* "Of course, I did." It took an act of God to prevent me from crawling across seats 7 D & E and strangling him for his utter ineptitude and inability to acknowledge that our colicky baby would want the one stuffed animal that soothes him to sleep, or that since we are going to a sun-drenched beach yes, I did, in fact, remember to pack their swimsuits along with the special earplugs the Ear, Nose and Throat doctor fitted to Cameron's pint-sized ears because the tubes in his ears prevent him from swimming in the ocean.

I speculate that Dan didn't help organize and pack not because he didn't care; it just wasn't worth his time. If I complained about his lack of assistance, he breezily suggested, "If we forgot anything, we'll just buy it when we get there." How could a man who persistently reminded me that we're on a budget, interrogated me each time I went to Target and, I suspect, installed a GPS tracking devise on my Master Card possibly hint that we just run out and buy forgotten unmentionables? More troublesome than his self-regulated budget demands, however, with which even he didn't comply (because Fantasy Football fees are always in the budget don't ya know), was the mere idea that I might forget the necessary comforts for my baby, which heavily contributed to my postpartum anxiety. What were the chances the hotel gift shop had a yellow, giraffe-encrusted Carter blanket circa 2001? Or the Gymboree stuffed monkey from 2004?

Asking for assistance required me to explain why each child required a different wattage night-light or where the thermometer and Vaseline were stored. And like most mothers, I found myself mumbling, "Just get the fuck out of the way. I'll do it myself."

I want to be the easy-going mom, I really do. I see the other moms. The ones who wake up two hours earlier than their kids, even if that means 3:30 a.m., to get their exercise and shower in before their darlings are up. The moms who don't care that raspberry jelly is smeared into the wall and one chicken nugget has fossilized in the corner of the family room. The ones who proudly drive minivans overflowing with Cheez-its and widowed socks and make spaghetti from scratch. The ones "making memories" by crafting their way through life with hot glue guns, scrapbooks and colored sand on the kitchen floor.

But I'm not that mom. I'm predisposed to anxiety and depression and despite my best efforts to chill out, motherhood exacerbates worry, concern and agitation. I'm the mom who washes curtains and slipcovers weekly. I neurotically sweep the kitchen floor because I don't want to feel like I'm trekking through the Sahara on my way to the refrigerator for a snack. I clean and organize and tidy all day long to maintain some kind of control over my surroundings. Stains make me furious, hot dogs and grapes worry me to death, and wrestling of any kind petrifies me with the (admittedly slight) possibility a spinal cord injury might permanently paralyze my child. While missed naps and dropped snacks singularly aren't catastrophic, they create cranky, little assholes. And cranky, little assholes make me edgy. You know what takes the edge off? Medicine. And alcohol. Or medicine soaked in alcohol.

In the grand scheme of parenthood, a spilled glass of milk or speeding earthbound asteroid *shouldn't* send me running to the medicine or liquor cabinet, but it does. Sometimes I run crying and screaming, other times I crawl sluggishly, leaving deep claw marks in the hardwood floors. I worry about everything from lead paint and vaccines to anthrax and earthquakes. From car accidents and kidnappings to nut allergies and school shootings. Terrorists, global warming and the Mayan calendar! The anxiety is as vast as the devastating possibilities themselves.

When Felicity was the size of a mere kiwi in my uterus, I scored a shabby-chic lavender bench to compliment her lilac nursery. It sat in her nursery for a wee 48 hours before I spied a termite push its viscous little head through one of the "antique" wooden slats. Dan was traveling for business, so I hurled that plague-ridden bench down two flights of stairs and out into the driveway, called the Center for Disease Control crying about termites gnawing away at my unborn baby's flesh and promptly had our brand-new house tented and fumigated in Dan's absence.

And that level of anxiety was *before* the baby was even out of my body.

Imagine my burden now with not one, but two children! And one is a boy!

Naturally, of all the twists and turns on this road we call motherhood, some incidents weigh heavier than others. While an unexplained rash, for example, may warrant a heightened level of awareness, I am abnormally composed. An open head wound, calm as a cucumber. But, something as insignificant as soggy Cheerios left in the diaper bag leaves me whimpering in the fetal position on the floor. The reality is it's more than just soggy Cheerios, because mothers are always thinking twelve steps ahead. Soggy Cheerios means the emergency snack is ruined and inedible which lead to a hungry, cranky asshole. The soggy Cheerios will certainly leak all over the diaper bag soiling backup clothes, which you absolutely need because it's Tuesday and Tuesday is Gymboree class which always causes an explosive blowout. You also need to run by the grocery store to pick up dinner and Oh! the dry-cleaning must be picked up by 5:00 p.m. and you don't have time to run home for extra clothes because if you did you might as well go in the house and nurse the baby since the Cheerios were ruined and if you do that he'll fall asleep. And if he falls asleep you can't put him back in the car seat because he would wake up crying so he'll need to nap in his crib which would make you miss the dry-cleaning and grocery store. So you just sit down and weep and ask your husband to pick up take-out, yet again, while crying something about a Cheerio into the muffled phone.

Every single incident has a consequence and the aftermath is often one, big spectacular domino stunt, each outwardly minor mishap toppling over the next block and the next until you are a polka-dot mess on the floor. A pooped-on car seat cover doesn't just mean extra laundry; it means that you're trapped in the house isolated and alone while your only car seat cover cycles through the washer and dryer causing you to miss afternoon coffee with a dear friend — your lifeline to staying alive. A premature nap in the car doesn't simply mean baby is up extra late; it means you'll be up all night too, with supplemental feedings, missing your early morning shower — the only one you'll get for three days.

Of all the speed bumps on Parenthood Lane (which often feels more like a dead end), lack of sleep may have the biggest impact on postpartum depression. Exhaustion cuts into you — shredding your sanity and robbing you of hope. Like a blade, fatigue slices through your ability to identify which bumps cause collisions and which are merely fender-benders on the road of motherhood. Meals, for example, are routine duties of child-rearing that should be approached lovingly, not as a conflict or catastrophe. However, it feels much more like a major defeat when an innocent child demands food immediately after you've cleaned the kitchen. I often find myself with clenched teeth and fists wondering, "Why the fuck is my child only hungry *after* I clean the kitchen?" while smashing plates onto the floor.

Genuine worry and trifling irritation mix together causing an overall state of exasperation. It's that lens and level of madness through which I view the world and the people around me. There are other things too — seemingly petty things — that grate on me.

Like Respecting Privacy

I could meander around my house for hours unnoticed, but the moment I go to the bathroom a child will undeniably penetrate the bathroom door and appear in front of me with a "necessary" question — though their father is mere feet away. Am I the only parent who can discern whether or not a child can have an extra chocolate chip cookie or go outside and play? I don't need to see your Minecraft city at this precise moment. And when, too, did the insertion of a tampon become an affair with its very own little audience? Yes, mommy *is* performing a magic trick. Poof! All gone. Now if I could only make *you* temporarily disappear while I finish wiping the hemorrhoids that are threatening to become a sizable vineyard on my rectum. 2004, by the way, would have produced a hearty Cab. Just sayin'.

Like Hypothetical Questions

What if someone just walked up to you and gave you a million dollars? What if pets could speak English like us? Would you rather be a fish or a dinosaur? Why is that man walking down the street? Where do you think he's going? Do you think animals are happy? What if you could rob a bank and not get caught? If you could have one superpower, what would it be?

And my personal favorite: Are we there yet? That one seems to always pop up while we are cruising 70-miles-an-hour down an eight-lane highway, which is extremely concerning to me. If we were, in fact, *there*, wouldn't we be stopped? Or at a very minimum not barreling down the freeway? Do my children lack such common sense that they are unaware of what *being there* means? I frequently respond with, "Yes, we're there. Get out." I will be awfully sorry if, one day, they open the car door and lurch from the safe confines of our speeding car. Serves 'em right, though. They need to learn what it means to arrive somewhere and be "there" — wherever "there" is.

They're so preoccupied asking stupid questions about our whereabouts that they don't even recognize when we do actually arrive "there." Countless times I've stood outside the car while my children sit, securely fastened into their seats staring blissfully out the window at my crumpled, red face. I want to scream, "We're *there*. Get the fuck out of the car now!"

I think painter and expressionist Edvard Munch was actually a woman — an exasperated mother, in fact — who painted the famous "The Scream" pastel while her children were incessantly chattering on and demanding notice. It wasn't Macaulay Culkin in "Home Alone" who patented that now-famous image of hands hugging an open-mouth scream; it was a shrieking mother. Perhaps even Edvard Munch. Or was it Edwina Munch? And screaming, so it seems, is only effective if you place your hands on your flushed cheeks and raise your voice several octaves. It's particularly effective, too, if you slide your fingers upward and rip hair from your temples — that really gets the kids' attention!

I pulled a lot of hair out during Cameron's earliest years. He went through an almost two-year phase where no matter what you told him to do, he'd fashion his thumb and forefinger into a gun, point it squarely at your face and say, "Phew! You're on fire!" Questions, statements, instructions — didn't matter — if he didn't like what you said, "Phew! You're on fire!" For nearly two years he was setting me ablaze. Oh, I was burnt up all right, over his relentless disobedience. Our parenting plan, although had only slightly changed to incorporate the *family bed* (hey, we were tired), had not budged from our no-spanking policy, which only left me saying, "You're lucky you're so cute." Had Cameron not been so adorable in his defiance, he might have not fared so well.

Having a boy the second time around was like nothing I ever expected. Felicity, being both the eldest and a girl, was a natural pleaser. Laid back, happy and compliant. Cameron, on the other hand, was loud, rebellious, grumpy and consistently dirty. Felicity had a conscious and would be genuinely disheartened if she'd done something ill mannered throughout the day. She couldn't fall asleep without first sulking up to my side of the bed to apologize for whatever grievance she had. On the contrary, Cameron spent many play dates confined to his bedroom for not apologizing for something he'd blatantly done or said. He's a boy; he didn't care. He once knocked on the neighbor's door and said, "I want to jump on your trampoline, but I don't want you to join me." He's honest, I'll give him that, but I wasn't prepared for his lack of niceties. Nor was I prepared for how much boys climb. They climb on everything. Everywhere. All the time. Ninety percent of parenting a boy is saying, "Please get down." I fear for his life daily — whether from me slaying him or from carelessly falling to his untimely death.

My friend has a theory that postpartum depression is more common among moms who have cesarean births. She might be right, but I suspect a truer notion is the older the mother is at the time of birth, the more likely she is to experience anxiety and depression. I was over 30 years old when I had my first child and 33 by the second. I theorize that once you've had a successful career, reached a certain level of authority and appreciate having subordinates, that having teeny, tiny people who don't do what you say is somewhat aggravating. Maddening even. I would certainly never ask a supervising attorney *why* I had to do something, regardless of how inconvenient or stupid I thought I it was. I suspect he'd say something like, "Because I said so," in which case I'd quickly comply since I understand the hierarchy of a law firm. Yet, as the CEO of my home, no one listens to a damn thing *I* say, especially not "Because I said so." It's frightening, really. I think *I had a career. I was in charge of a lot of people. Grown people. I have better negotiating skills than you. I'm taller than you!* Yet I can't make them do anything. I bet if I were a badge-toting, gun-slinging FBI Agent mom those little fuckers would mind me.

I'm over it. Really.

They say don't be your child's friend, be their parent. Why? Kids don't listen to their parents; they listen to their friends. I suspect teen moms have it a little easier in some respects — they've never been in position of authority and, frankly, they're not that far removed from being children themselves. As an adolescent mom, I speculate, "Go clean your room," resonates as friendly advice. *Everyone's totally doing it!* That's why parents need to appreciate and use texting lingo — to order kids around in a new cool and hip way. For example, "I'll b L8, u *vin? mke ur own dnr," very obviously translates to "I'll be late. If you are starving, make your own dinner." And, "SMH @ study L8R, now," clearly means, "I'm shaking my head at you studying later, study now!"

It's a slippery slope this motherhood gig. They say it gets infinitely harder with each progressive phase. I have yet to grasp how my children becoming respectful, independent, employable citizens is going to be tougher. I can already see positive changes as we enter the middle school years. While Felicity occasionally erupts through the bathroom door to tell me something inconsequential, it doesn't grate on me nearly as badly as it used to; I'm just thankful she's still talking to me in her thorny teenage years. No more sleepless nights (at least not until they get driver's licenses), colicky babies or explosive diapers. No more apple-bobbing breast-feeding renditions, although I'm considering taking up pumping and dumping just to rid myself of these twenty extra pounds. Cameron no longer mimics shooting me in the face with blazing fire; now I periodically get shot with a Nerf bullet, but that's purely accidental, or so he says. Cameron too has outgrown his grumpy phase and morphed into a sweet, loving, and agreeable young man who, incidentally, can take a shit anywhere and without *artificial stimulation*. I might not be the perfect mother, but in my eyes (and I'm certain his, too) that's even better and a relief that I don't have to follow him to college "encouraging" his bowels.

I am now free of anti-depressants (as of the writing of this chapter and, fingers crossed, still at the time of you reading it) and I feel happy, optimistic and buoyant about my maternal future. Perhaps, in part, because I'm in the sweet spot of parenting; the kids are fun and thoughtful, capable yet not fiercely independent. September 11th may have hijacked more than just my dreams of being the perfect mother, but let's be honest, my kids didn't drive me crazy; I was already there with "1989" stamped in the upper right corner, remember? Despite getting my ticket repeatedly stamped on the crazy train, life has graciously afforded me a leisurely U-turn and I am so thankful that I weathered this daunting and dreadful postpartum depression.

Nevertheless, I am not naïve enough to believe there won't be a sniper lurking in the Target parking lot or camouflaged as a Starbucks barista waiting to take aim at me in my weakest moments. Anxiety and worry are undoubtedly fibers tightly knit in the fabric of my life, but so are love and laughter. As I reflect on those peculiar days in New Life Hospital, I recognize that it is laughter, particularly, that has helped me traverse this miracle of child rearing. It was there, in the mental ward strangely enough, where I learned to value humor, embrace life and raise my children with love, laughter and just the right amount of crazy.

Parenting's greatest moments come from relishing in the journey itself — the brief roadside moments of happiness, joy, celebration and growth — more than the final destination. It's about acceptance, resilience, and surviving, healing and, above all else, unconditional love. Love of your children as well as yourself. Love of your darkness and brightness. Sometimes you have to walk through extreme darkness to truly appreciate the brilliance of light; in motherhood, the light is often a flashing beacon of sanity. It's a faint glow leading you out of the despair and loneliness towards a destination of hope and happiness. I would have never guessed my path would be what it's been, but I wouldn't trade it for the whole world. And as far as the destination, I suspect when I get there — wherever "there" is — it will be an exasperated, yet proud maternal moment when I can say to my children as they sit in the backseat of my car, "We're there. Get the fuck out now!"

Twelve

THE MARATHON

I began 2009 feeling more optimistic than in previous years as the kids entered a more joyous and self-sufficient phase. Fresh with maternal freedom, I felt positive, self-assured and brave. As I embraced my life and its renewed journey, I wondered how I could harness that courage and adventurous sensation. In a bold act of personal heroism, I registered for a full marathon although at the time I couldn't run one uninterrupted mile.

I hired a professional running coach, trained for five months and began to document my journey. These are the weekly email journals detailing that ghastly experience.

Date: February 14, 2009
From: Leigh Baker
To: Friends and Family
Subject: Marathon Training - Journal #1

Hey y'all,

OK, all of you know me fairly well, so you know I'm the laziest piece of shit you'll ever meet. I will avoid exercise at all costs. Seriously, I would rather sit on the couch and eat of bag of Cheetos than do anything remotely athletic. Well, long story short, I woke up on New Year's Day (apparently, not hung over enough) and decided I would register for a marathon. Yes, a real one. *Running* the marathon, not handing out Jello shots at the finish line. Nevertheless, I am in serious training mode. OK, not *that* serious. I drink several mochas a day, eat lots of pizza and have a bottle of wine each night, but I also run five times a week. I hired a running coach, she tells me what to do and I do it. She told me to run nine miles today. Lucky for her, she gives me these little nuggets of information via email otherwise I'd have to slap her (and try not to spill my wine). I just ran 9.25 miles. All at once. Without stopping. I swear. I think am experiencing what must be described as the "runner's high" because I feel AMAZING!

I have to go take a nap now.

Love,
Leigh

Date: February 21, 2009
From: Leigh Baker
To: Friends and Family
Subject: Marathon Training - Journal #2

So, last week during my "runner's high" I excitedly informed you all that I'm training for a marathon. Yeah, well, the runner's high is fucking gone. I'd rather just be high now. (Although at this point in my life I've never actually *been* high, I'm certain it feels better than my current state.) I ran 11 miles today. I was hoping someone's dog would attack me on the trail so I could stop running. I even tried to give some kid ten bucks to run me over with his bicycle. I think I lost one kneecap and I might have had a mild heart attack around mile ten, but I'm too lazy to drive myself to the Emergency Room to find out.

The good news is I found a GU flavor that's tolerable. For you non-marathoners (which would be most of my friends because I don't usually associate with the healthy running type), there's this shit out there that you eat while you run to give you energy. It comes in a cute little colorful packet (similar to a pack of Skittles, but tastes nothing like Skittles) and is basically shit/motor-oil/mud that's packed with caffeine, carbohydrates and God knows what else. I've been testing out various

GU flavors, and today I tried mint chocolate chip. It was pretty good. Not Baskin-Robbins good, but good. Now if they could squeeze some hot fudge, whipped cream, nuts and a cherry into that little shit-bag I might like it more.

My reward for running 11 miles is to go pig out on Mexican food. There is a God. Farewell for now.
Running in Raleigh,
Leigh

Date: March 1, 2009
From: Leigh Baker
To: Friends and Family
Subject: Marathon Training - Journal #3

Weather Report: 46 Degrees, pouring rain, occasional gusts of wind (yay!)
Goal: 13 Miles

I just finished reading this hysterical book called *The Non-Runners Guide to Marathon Running*. It's about a couch potato (like me) who decides to run a marathon and tell her pathetic and funny journey. In the book, her running partner is a girl she calls Chipper Jen. Chipper Jen is this runner girl who's freakishly excited about all things running. Well, Dan and I set out for our freezing, rainy run this morning, and we'd barely gotten started when we passed our very own Chipper Jen. This freak came running toward us waving uncontrollably with a big toothy grin yelling, "Hi! Oh my God! Good morning! Have a great run!"

I looked at Dan and said, "What the fuck was her problem?"

Somewhere around mile three, a bird shit on me. It strategically hit the front of my chest. During my frequent bouts of self-doubt and heart attack pains, I typically end up hunched over while I run/shuffle, so the bird crap on the front of my chest provided a nice focal point for me for several miles. Thank you, kind bird.

Not long after that, a gust of wind blew a branch off of a tree and hit Dan in the neck. I thought I was going to pee myself from laughing so hard. That little burst of joy carried me at least another quarter of a mile, but then, maybe as payback from karma, I stepped in a huge mound of goose poop. We run on a trail around a lake and through the greenway system, where there are hundreds of geese. Those are stubborn little fuckers; they don't even pretend to care if they're in your way. After I stepped in the goose poop, I had to run/shuffle while wiping the poop off my shoe without slowing down (because that would be a complete stop).

Two miles and two nasty GU pouches later, I began to hallucinate, probably because those pouches don't prevent starvation. There was a huge *thing* in the middle of the trail. I know it sounds all Dr. Suessy just calling it a "thing," but there's no other way to describe it except to say I thought it was a Butterball Turkey. I told Dan, "Sweet. Someone left us a Butterball Turkey." As we approached the thing, I sadly discovered it was not a Butterball, although I still couldn't make out what it was. The mystery of it, however, kept me going for another half of a mile. We reached the halfway mark and turned around to head back to our starting point. The rain was pouring, we were drenched, Dan's neck was bleeding and I was hungry. We passed the Butterball Turkey thing again, and although I still couldn't figure out what the hell it was, I thought I smelled funnel cake. I then began to have visions similar to Alex the Lion from Madagascar. Alex, if you recall, was famished and fantasized that Marty's butt was a big, juicy steak. I couldn't get that movie and image out of my mind. I typically run about five steps behind Dan, and today I was close to biting his ass on several occasions. I didn't bite him, but continued to run in my delirious condition.

Miles seven through thirteen were a blur. A strange white foam was building up on my knees and I couldn't decide if it was goose poop, bird shit, rain or snow, or some awful bony plasma froth seeping from my kneecaps. I never figured that one out either.

Well, after several miles of hopping over puddles and dodging geese, I made it. I ran a total of 13.07 miles. All at once. Without stopping. In the pouring freaking rain. That was the single lamest thing I've ever done. (Except for that time in college when I thought I could disassemble Dan's futon, wash it and put it together again.)

Running sucks. But I feel amazing!

Love,

Leigh

Date: March 7, 2009
From: Leigh Baker
To: Friends and Family
Subject: Marathon Training - Journal #4

Weather Report: 77 degrees and sunny
Goal: 8 Miles

It's fucking hot out there. Since I've been training, it's either been raining, snowing, or just plain cold. As a matter of fact, it snowed earlier this week for two of my runs. Today was beautiful and sunny. First order of business: ditch the gloves, fleece and thermals for some shorts. Let me just say that my thighs were not meant to wear shorts. I do, however, favor the skort. Feels like a short, looks like skirt and is typically flattering on most body types. So I slipped into my fashionable skort and headed out for my run.

During the first mile I thought, *God, it's so nice out today.* By mile two, I was more like, *Fuck, it's hot out here.* It was at that point when I accidentally spit a loogie on myself. Dan enjoyed that. By mile three I had to pee so bad I hopped off the trail and ducked into a McDonald's to go potty. Mmm, the smell of Big Macs. Momma's home! I knew I should've shoved a few dollars into my bra. (I wonder if they could make a Big Mac flavored GU? I'm writing someone about that.) Well, that little pit stop made it seriously hard to get my rhythm back. If you saw me, you'd wonder what kind of rhythm I really had to begin with. But trust me. It was hard to get back into a rhythm.

This week's run felt so much harder than last week's. I was hot and tired and had a huge wedgie from my skort. It was the worst kind of wedgie — a front wedgie. A vagina-wedgie. Let's call it a veggie (if you know what I mean). So my veggie was annoying me, my thighs were rubbing together and I was certain I would catch on fire from the flames shooting out of my crotch. Although I never did actually catch fire, at the very least I'm sure I gave myself a rash and a yeast infection.

After McDonald's, we passed a Boy Scout table set up in the middle of nowhere. Most people know the Girl Scouts sell cookies and the Boy Scouts sell candy bars, so as I ran closer to them I thought, *Why are the Boy Scouts on this trail?* and then I thought, *Are those little fuckers selling candy bars to runners and bikers on an exercise trail, of all places?* Seriously, that's just mean. And bad parenting for whichever tribe leader bitch thought that was a good idea (though again, I wished I'd shoved a dollar into my bra). Turns out it was not a candy bar stand, they were just being "green" and picking up all the trash on the nature trail. I wished they were selling candy bars instead.

Did I mention that Dan enjoyed some Amber Ale last night? Yeah, so Mr. Fart Machine had his own rhythm during our entire run. Remember how I'm usually five to ten spaces *behind* him? I don't know if he was trying to make me run faster or just kill me. Needless to say, it didn't kill me, which is so unfortunate because I was hoping it would. I really felt like dying out there today. My music was killing me, too; I really need to update my iPod playlist, because if I hear Coldplay one more fucking time I'm going to shoot myself. I considered switching over to Felicity's playlist, which is also on my iPod, but the Jonas Brothers' *Burnin' Up* only made me think of my burning veggie more. I was trying to run, pick the skort out of my ass and vagina and not let my legs touch all at the same time, but I couldn't figure out how to run with my legs four feet apart. Plus, I had already perfected my run/shuffle.

The last several miles were brutal, but I did it. I have a blister on my pinky toe and I need a massage and a fruity cocktail.

Love,

Steady Betty (the nickname I gave myself today because I can't seem to run any faster or slower — I just go.)

⌒

Date: March 15, 2009
From: Leigh Baker
To: Friends and Family
Subject: Marathon Training - Journal #5

Weather Report: 39 degrees and pouring rain
Goal: 14 Miles

The bad news — it was cold and rainy. The good news — I didn't have to run in shorts that gave me a severe veggie. I'm so sorry to disappoint you all, but no veggie tales today. I did, however, shit myself on mile 12.

Just kidding.

I almost did, though.

I bundled up in cold-weather gear and headed out for my miserable run. Dan and I pulled up to the lake, walked about ten feet and I said, "Dammit, I've got to pee." I figured, *Surely there are no other idiots out here today running, so I'll just squat right here on the trail* (which was under a bridge and in a tunnel of sorts). So I squatted and waited. And waited. And waited. The chill in the air was a tad too cold and gave me stage fright. Just as I started to piss all over the sidewalk, this huge black guy came running through the tunnel toward us. My faithful running partner and husband, Dan, jumped in front of me to either protect my privacy or protect the man's eyes from the glow coming off my big white ass in the tunnel. He ran up to us and said to Dan, as if he didn't even see me pissing in the middle of the trail, "Terrible day to run, huh?" Dan goes, "Uh, yeah." After that little encounter we started to run. And run. And run.

I know this doesn't make any sense, but it's actually easier to run in the cold rain than in the heat, so despite the frigid air, this was a little easier than last week's sweltering run. Again, jumping over mud puddles and dodging goose poop provided a slight distraction from the weather. We tried out a new route today to make up for the extra miles I needed to log; you can only run around a two-mile lake so many times before it gets old.

I should say we *attempted* to run a new route, but we got lost around mile five or six. The greenway trails are not adequately marked, which makes it hard to have any idea where you're going. It's annoying. Someone: fix that. Anyway, we got lost, backtracked, got lost again, backtracked again. After three or four attempts to get on the right trail, we decided to just run through some old neighborhoods downtown.

It was a beautiful neighborhood with hundred-year-old trees and homes with huge brick porches and magnolia trees to die for. Knowing my run/shuffle pace, Dan figured we should run for about an hour and a half, then turn around and run back. That would give us three hours of straight running and hopefully get us to our 14-mile goal.

Yeah, that didn't work. I ran for three hours straight all right, but somehow came up short on my mileage. I don't know if it was the weather slowing me down, my fat ass slowing me down or the fact that we got lost a million times.

Things were pretty uneventful from about mile six to mile 12 — I think I zoned out or fell asleep. I did, however, notice that I neglected to put on the right bra. These wardrobe malfunctions are really getting on my nerves. How am I supposed to know what to run in? I never run. Now, I wouldn't typically describe my boobs as bouncy. Non-existent and pathetic? Yes. But, bouncy? Never. However, running in a bad bra was making my little girls bounce, so as I ran down the hills I cupped my boobs as if to protect myself. Clearly they weren't going to give me black eyes, but it was a tad uncomfortable nonetheless. So, picture me flailing down hills, holding my boobies in my completely stupid running form. If I were naked, it would've looked like I was running from a burning building. Slowly. So pathetic.

During that time, someone started knocking on my back door.

Here's my usual morning routine: wake up, have one cup of coffee, maybe two (anything more than two is asking for trouble), force myself to eat breakfast, poop, leave for my run. On this particular morning, I might have had three cups of coffee, not enough food, and no poop. Believe me, I tried. Is it wrong to pray to God for a good poop? (By the way, this is not the first time I've prayed about poop. After you squeeze out a baby, taking a crap is probably the number one scariest thing you will ever encounter. Pushing a ten-pound baby out your hoo-ha is nothing compared to the tears you will shed during your first postpartum shit.) Where was I? Oh, yeah, praying for a good crap. Well, God must have been busy with starving children and all, because he didn't quite get my request until 11 miles into my run. In case you didn't know this, it is physically impossible to run while you have to take a shit. Seriously. Try it.

By the time we got back to the lake and eventually the car, I was running/shuffling in a way that looked like I was walking over hot coals. I don't even know what I was doing because my feet hurt so badly. Dan and I came to an abrupt stop, ripped our iPod headphones out and I yelled, "I have to take the biggest shit!" and Dan replied, "Yeah, well my left nut is about to pop!" We hobbled back to the car, with Dan complaining the whole way that his left nut might be permanently damaged.

He said, "I swear. My left nut has been pinned in between my hipbone and rib for at least six miles. I tried to take my glove off and reach in there to reposition it, but my fucking glove was so wet it was stuck and I couldn't get it off." I died laughing. He was in serious pain though. He kept saying, "Leigh, you don't fucking understand. My nut is going to POP THE FUCK OPEN! I'm going to have one nut for the rest of my life. Seriously. I can't feel my nut. It's stuck in my fucking hip joint."

Oh… good times. Good times.

Anyway, we made it home and thawed out. I took the mother shit and Dan dug his left nut out of his rib cage. It was a beautiful day.

Love,

Steady Betty & Righty

Date: March 22, 2009
From: Leigh Baker
To: Friends and Family
Subject: Marathon Training - Journal #6

Weather Report: 40 degrees and sunny (finally)
Goal: 14 Miles

I just want to be clear about one thing in case there's any confusion: I hate running. No, seriously. It sucks ass.

First of all, I didn't think I was going to be able to type this journal entry until the year 2020 when my body stops hurting. Here's a short list of what aches at this moment: my left pinky toe, my left second biggest toe, both feet, ankles, my spleen, my shins, both of my legs, I cannot even begin to describe the pain in my knees, all 206 bones in my body, my epidermis, my large intestines, my cornea, my gall bladder and everything else either inside, outside, under, over or even remotely related to my body.

And here is what's getting on my nerves at this particular moment: Dan. He is supposedly great at math, but keeps fucking with the mileage (and me). According to the Raleigh Parks and Recreation Official Greenway map, I ran 15.8 miles today. According to the map of Dan Baker, I ran "about 14 miles." He thinks the Official map must have been printed wrong. Fuck him. I ran 15.8 miles.

I have to admit, it was a beautiful day to go for a run, if you're into that sort of shit. The weather was perfect. I carbed up the night before and ate a good breakfast, although I still couldn't poop before we left the house (thankfully, I didn't have to poop while running this time, either). Because the weather was a tad hotter than I was used to, I used up all the liquids in my fuel belt by the halfway mark. Ugh. I was screwed. By the time we turned around to head back, my body was already so sore. Strangely enough, my hip and pubic bone were hurting the most, and I thought my uterus was about to fall out of my hot pocket. Either that or I was about to birth the Steak Fajitas I chowed down the night before. My whole midsection hurt.

Running cannot be good for you. These people who say running is the best exercise clearly don't run. They're like those people who say money can't buy happiness. Who the fuck are these people? They're clearly broke and don't know what the hell they're talking about. Of *course* money buys happiness.

Around mile ten, two 70-year-old ladies came flying by me. Fucking bitches. Then about a mile later, I was hunched over in my usual state, staggering along, when this old man on a bike says, "How ya doin'?"

I barked back, "I'm fucking tired. What does it look like?" I felt kind of bad about yelling at him, but seriously, any dumbass could see I wasn't having a good time.

I think I get delirious on these long runs. At one point I had a great idea and yelled up to Dan, who was at least 40 yards ahead of me, "Do you think I could wear Heelys (those stupid little sneakers with wheels in the bottom that kids wear to whiz around you in the grocery store) in the marathon?" I don't think he heard me, but I laughed my ass off.

Around that time, Dan started saying, "We'll be there before you know it." He must have said that 25 times before I screamed, "Guess what? WE'RE NOT THERE AND I FUCKING KNOW IT!" I was so mad. Eventually, I just came to a complete stop and starting crying. I just started bawling like a big baby. Dan was like, "What the hell is wrong with you? Keep running — only two miles to go!" I couldn't even speak to him. I just stood in the middle of the trail crying, but I found the strength to start running again. I ran a few hundred yards, then stopped and cried some more. I dug deeper for some more strength, ran another hundred yards. Stopped. Cried. (Just repeat that scenario in your mind for about 15 minutes.) Dan kept yelling, "We'll be there before you know it." FUCK OFF, YOU ASSHOLE.

Then it happened. I had a *Forest Gump* moment. I was determined to get through the last mile or two, even if it was going to kill me. I had all kinds of visions in my head. *The Biggest Loser* triumph, Rocky Balboa running up the stairs, Whitney Houston singing at the top of her lungs with her sweaty-ass self. I was going to make it! I put my head down and just went for it. I ran as fast as I could. I blew past Dan. I blew past someone on a bike. I blew past two skinny bitches running. I was on fire.

This is it! I'm going to sprint all the way back to the car. I can do this. God, this is exactly what the marathon will be like. I will hit rock bottom, I will almost fail — then I will find the strength that has always been hiding within me. I'll run around the corner and see the finish line, and I'll sprint while all my friends and family and kids cheer me on. "GO MOMMY! GO MOMMY! GO MOMMY!" Oh, it will be great. I raaaaaaaaaannnnnnnnnnnnn like the wind.

Then SCREEEEEEEEEEEECH. I stopped and started crying again.

OK, so no Rocky Balboa/Whitney Houston moment. But I did run 15.8 miles today. I have no idea how I'm going to run that whole marathon; if any of you have a heart, you will start praying for me now. Seriously. Call your pastor, your friends, and your neighbors. Start a weekly prayer vigil because I don't know how on earth I'm supposed to run 26.2 miles all at once. If you haven't realized yet, I don't think things through very well before committing to them. I have learned my lesson.

By the way, next weekend I'm running the Raleigh Rocks Half Marathon. Wish me luck.
Love,
Steady Betty

Date: March 22, 2009
From: Leigh Baker
To: Friends and Family
Subject: Marathon Training - Journal #7

Today was the Raleigh Rocks Half Marathon. For those of you who don't know, a half marathon is 13.1 miles. So obviously my goal for today was to complete 13.1 miles.

Weather was forecasted earlier in the week for 50 degrees, rain, thunderstorms and possible hail. Nice. But God was looking out for us because the weather was 60 degrees and clear. It was, however, very *humid*. Yuck.

I skipped the coffee this morning in an effort to curb the urge to shit midway through my run. I think that was a smart choice. Dan and I drove downtown bright and early to find a parking spot; my running coach had told me to run a one-mile warm-up prior to the race. *What?* Why the hell would I run a whole mile *before* the race? That didn't make any sense to me at all. Apparently, it made sense to a lot of other people though, because there were dozens of people running up and down the streets of downtown Raleigh getting their warm-up in before the race. These people are freaks. But, I figured my running coach knows what she's talking about, so I did a little quarter-mile jaunt around a few blocks and called it good enough. We hit the porta-potties then headed toward the starting line. I saw my running coach. She shoved a granola bar down her throat, wished me luck and headed toward the front of the pack. Dan and I made our way to the middle of the pack and just waited for the excitement to begin.

It felt like an eternity waiting for the race to start. Shortly before we started, it looked like a mosh pit with everyone jumping up and down getting loose. I surveyed my competition and thought, *I'm fucked.* After about ten minutes of huddling together with other runners and wannabes, they sounded a loud horn. *Yay, we're off,* I thought. I immediately ran into the back of a few people. Oops. My bad. That wasn't the "go" buzzer. That was the "on your mark, get set" buzzer. Then, about 30 seconds later the "go" buzzer sounded. OK, *now* we're off.

The first few miles were overwhelming. Everyone was bumping into each other, trying to get out into their own space, chitchatting, laughing, hootin' and hollerin', stomping on each other. It was distracting. I wished I'd brought my iPod to drown out the noise. I also didn't appreciate everyone flying past me. I thought, *Well, shit. Where are all these people coming from?* Every single person registered for this half marathon must have passed me. I kept saying to Dan, "Please tell me there is someone behind me. I don't want to be the *very* last person."

After about two miles, I was sweating to death; it was very hard to run in the humidity. After all, I'd been running in the freezing cold for the last three months. The only consolation was that everyone around me was drenched, too.

Let me just say, there are a lot of weird people who run marathons. Runners come in all shapes and sizes. I've discovered that runners fall into distinct categories, much like Santa's reindeer. There's Dasher — those who run out of the gate too fast and think they're actually going to sustain that pace and win. There's Dancer — the 50-year-old ladies who do hot yoga and try to kid themselves into thinking they're still 25. Prancer — the gay guys who wear skin-tight running shirts, shorty shorts and have shaved all evidence of body hair. Vixen — according to the dictionary, a "female fox." These are the 22-year-old bitches with great bodies who look good running and don't even break a sweat. There's Comet — the naturally fast runner who actually does win the race. Donner is German for thunder — these are the obese people running *and* passing me, bless their hearts. Blitzen — the 22-year-old hung-over fraternity boys who roll out of bed and run the alcohol off. And then, of course, there's Rudolph, the pathetic little fawn everyone laughs at, is not allowed to play in the running games and thinks he's the most worthless in the bunch. That would be me. Although, Rudolph proves he has many talents. He can navigate quite well in bad climate conditions (again, me) and surprises everyone by being the star of the show (hopefully me).

At mile three, we saw this guy run off the course, duck into a Mini-Mart and grab a Red Bull. Seriously? Dude, it's only mile three. That's not going to get you through the next ten miles. What an idiot. Around that time I noticed a woman running slightly behind me and breathing very loudly. I kept checking on her to make sure she was OK. Later, Dan told me he thought that was *me* breathing. He said to himself, "Oh, shit. We're only at mile three and Leigh sounds like shit. She's not going to make it to the finish line." That woman kept the same pace with me for much of the race; I continued to check on her, but eventually her inhale/exhale gasps of death lead me into a nice rhythm. Thanks, lady.

At mile five, my running coach breezed past us in the opposite direction, heading back toward the finish line. Damn, she's fast. Maybe I should have done that one-mile warm-up after all.

Because it's a tradition in the Raleigh Rocks Half Marathon, there were live bands along the route playing music. I don't know where the hell they found these so-called bands, but they were awful; out of about five groups, two were just OK. The others were basically some Deadheads who pulled up to the side of the road, dragged an amp and a guitar out of their hatchback and rocked out. One of the worst bands had a groupie out there dancing and screaming like a lunatic. (See above description: she was definitely a Dancer. Perhaps she forgot to register for the race.) Anyway, the music was comical. I thought it would inspire me to keep going through the tough miles, but it was a joke. No wonder everyone broke the race rules and brought iPods.

The race wasn't even half over before we heard the first ambulance, right after we passed the old cougar lady and sucky band. That's also when Dan admitted that he'd had to take a shit for the last three miles. We spotted a porta-potty by the cow pasture we were running through, but there was already a line of runners waiting to drop their kids off at the pool. Dan kept slogging along, hopeful he'd be able to hold it until the next porta-potty, but there wasn't one. Ever. We ran along the State Fairgrounds where there was lots of traffic. Drivers honked and shouted lots of words of encouragement (about the marathon, not Dan's poop). That was cool.

At mile eight, I started my fucking period. I looked like a slaughtered pig running through a crowded Farmer's Market. That is all I'm going to say about that. It was de-scusting. But what's a runner girl to do? So, I just kept running.

Pretty soon we entered the North Carolina Museum of Art grounds. That was a beautiful run. We ran along a greenway trail around the museum, and through some strange sculptures. Among the sculptures was a huge, 60-foot tall corn on the cob. I don't know how else to describe it, except that it looked like a five-story-high half-eaten Cajun corn on the cob. Luckily, that scared Dan's poop back into his biscuits.

The next stretch was full of hills. I did great on the hills, no stopping or huffing and puffing. I just tackled them like a real runner. Toward the end of the museum trail was another "band" — a 23-year-old guy in full Scottish kilt get-up, playing the bagpipes. Now, don't get me wrong, the bagpipes are cool. At a funeral. Dan said, "This is weird. I only associate the bagpipes with death. I hope this doesn't mean something." I glanced back to see if heavy breather lady was OK. She was.

After the hills I felt a little tired, but I knew the rest of the way was flat and I was in the home stretch. I started passing all the people who'd dashed out of the starting line; those idiots were all slowing down or walking. Watch out, Steady Betty coming through! Dan's left nut was acting up a tad bit and making him nervous, but since his urge to shit subsided following the huge corn on the cob sighting, he was feeling good, too. As we approached the last few miles, people started appearing to cheer us on. The fans who cracked me up were the ones sitting in their lawn chairs, reading the paper and sipping coffee. Occasionally they would look up from their paper and yell, "Good job." It was such an effort on their part and I appreciated it so very much. Once we entered downtown again, all the breakfast restaurants were opening. The aroma went from piss, beer and incense to bacon, eggs and onions. It was a beautiful thing. I know that made Dan run faster.

During the very last mile, these two girls running alongside us were almost to their breaking point. One of them said, "I'm so sore. I just want to sit down and cry." The other girl agreed that sounded like a much better plan than running the last mile.

I turned around and said to them, "If it makes you girls feel any better, I started my fucking period over five miles ago." They surveyed my body, which looked like it had been stabbed multiple times. That whipped their asses into shape. They died laughing and thanked God they weren't me. See? Things could always be worse. I feel good knowing I helped them find some perspective.

As we came around the last corner downtown, we saw the finish line, all the screaming fans and the headliner band (whatever that was) and we were pumped. We finished strong. I estimated it would take about three hours to complete the race. My goal was two hours and 50 minutes. We completed it in about two hours and 30 minutes. As we ran across the finish line they handed us fake medals and Dan yelled, "I've got to take a shit!" and I yelled, "I need a fucking tampon!"

We chugged some water, ate some oranges and bagels, and hobbled to the car a few blocks away. When we got to the car I grabbed my camera and asked this old lady walking down the street if she would mind taking our photo. She said, "Oh did you just run in that race?"

I proudly confirmed and Dan said all grumpily, "We don't have to put these medals on for the photo do we?"

The sweet old lady said, "Oh you got a medal? What place did you come in?"

Dan and I laughed, and I said, "First and second."
Love,
Steady Betty

Date: March 22, 2009
From: Leigh Baker
To: Friends and Family
Subject: Marathon Training - Journal #8

Weather Report: 70 and sunny
Goal: 16 Miles

There seem to be some recurring challenges I face each week: weather complications, wardrobe choices and bowel movements.

My friend gave me some Body Glide (not to be confused with Astroglide) for today's run. Now that it's getting warmer outside, I need to dress lighter. Less coverage equals more chaffing. Body Glide looks like deodorant, and you rub it onto all potential chaffing areas. I experimented with it last week during the half marathon, when I was wearing shorts and a short-sleeve shirt. I had no chaffing issues after that race, so I thought it was a great product. Dan opted to not use the Body Glide last week and paid for it big time. Apparently, for male runners, the big chaffing area is their nipples. Nice, huh? I don't quite understand this phenomenon. Why, of all things, do their nipples get irritated? Why wouldn't it be their necks around the collar, or the armholes or something else? After last week's half marathon, Dan's nipples were so chaffed they were bleeding. I felt a little bad for him, but secretly thought to myself, *Now you know what it's like to breastfeed*. Let's run 13 freakin' miles in circles, get dog-ass tired and delirious, cry once or twice along the way and start bleeding from our nipples, race home for a quick shower then make the kids lunch — yep, just like being a mom. Marathons must have been invented by women to make men feel just a little bit of the pain we go through each day as mothers.

Dan wasn't going to make the same mistake twice, but rather than load up on the Body Glide he opted for Band-Aids over his nipples. Unfortunately, our Band-Aid supply is getting low with Cameron still living at home so all he could find were Batman Band-Aids. So, Dan slapped some little Batman Band-Aids on his nipples and he was ready for our run. I, on the other hand, slathered myself in Body Glide. My wardrobe choice for today was compression capris, a sports bra and Nike tank top made of super see-through wicking material. I was very comfortable. The compression capris are awesome and they make my ass look great. If Dan ever discovers just how fucked up and crazy I really am and leaves me, this will be the outfit I wear to the clubs to pick up men: compression leggings.

Now let's discuss the bra situation. OK, every woman has that one thing she hates shopping for — jeans, a bikini. Mine is the bra. It's like a man trying on jock straps and not having a penis — it just doesn't fit right. Or shopping for a hat and not having a head. You get my point. You can't fill up something with nothing. Anyway, one of my major wardrobe problems has always been the bra. Since support is not on the top of my priority list, I've been wearing what they call, in the teen world, a bralette, or I wear a light yoga bra or bikini top. This week I went shopping for a real sports bra. It was exhausting and humiliating.

My main complaint with sports bras is that there's no clasp. You have to pull this entire contraption over your big head, try to maneuver your shoulders through it, then onto your body. I have a big-ass Doogie Howser head, one dislocated shoulder and no boobs. So trying on sports bras is painful, both emotionally and physically. Anyway, I managed to survive (although I lost one earring in the process and I'm pissed about that) and walk out with two new real sports bras.

Now, this might be just a little bit too much information (as if I've been so modest up until this point) but, apparently, I have silver dollar nipples that cannot be covered up. After I sent out last week's half marathon photo, my girlfriend Elizabeth responded with two words: nice nipples. I don't care how thick the fabric is, my nipples stick out, which I guess is why Elizabeth's husband accuses me of "smugglin' raisins." Anyway, I slipped (or pried myself) into my new sports bra and Dan said, "No matter how hard you try, there is no covering those things up." Sigh. So Dan, my new outfit, my eraser nipples and I headed out for a run.

We went on a slightly new route today. There were some hills I wasn't used to, but otherwise a nice run. After the majority of the hills were behind us, I began to feel a cramp in my hip/butt/leg. It came and went but didn't particularly concern me. While we ran through N.C. State's campus we saw all the college kids in their jammies and sweats roll out of bed to go get their coffee at 11:30 a.m. What a life. I miss the good old days.

Around mile ten, that cramp in my hip/butt came back and I had to take a short walk break. After my short walk break, I had a short run. Then another short walk break and a short run. Then a long walk break and short run. This went on for a good mile. Finally, Dan said, "Do you want me to run back and get the car?" Music to my ears. We decided this wasn't doing me any good, so I'd better walk it in before I really injured myself. I don't know what was worse, me walking it in or seeing him sprint off in front of me at his usual pace. I pleaded, "Could you at least wait until you're out of my eyesight before you start running so fast?" So off into the distance he ran as I hobbled along the path toward the car. My hip/butt cramp was hurting so bad I could barely walk, and had to drag my entire right leg behind me as I made my way down the sidewalk. I also discovered that I missed a few critical areas with the Body Glide. My armpits were burning. I tried to walk with my arms straight out to the side like a scarecrow so they wouldn't rub against my body, all the while dragging my right leg behind me. Dan was to meet me at the Museum, so I had to walk this way alone for a good two miles. It was embarrassing and painful. I looked like a complete idiot.

During my last little hike through the Museum trail, I saw these two little kids I know from school riding their bikes. Their parents are both E.R. doctors and I thought, *Awesome. I can ask the mom for help.* Well, it was dad duty that morning, and the dad doesn't really know me. I contemplated asking him for help. *Excuse me, Dillon's Dad? Could you please rub this cramp out of my ass cheek?* I don't think he would've done it and I didn't want to waste my breath asking; plus, if he said "no" I would've been pissed and possibly gotten violent on him in front of his children. So I scuttled past them like a scarecrow or an extra from Michael Jackson's *Thriller* video and hoped they didn't recognize me.

Dan made good time going to get the car. Bastard. By the way, if anyone saw a body splayed out on the sidewalk on Blue Ridge Road in front of the Museum, that was me. I couldn't help but lay my head down in shame as I waited for my ride. When Dan got there, I crawled into the car and cranked up the butt warmer in an effort to ease my cramp. He'd run the last four and half miles back to the car in like 25 minutes or something. Whatever.

Until next week, enjoy this photo of Dan.
As always,
Steady Betty

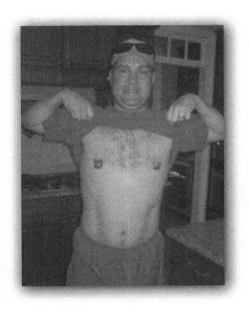

Date: April 11, 2009
From: Leigh Baker
To: Friends and Family
Subject: Marathon Training - Journal #9

I ran 18 miles today. Ouch.
   The End.
Love,
Leigh
P.S. I fucking hate running.

Date: March 22, 2009
From: Leigh Baker
To: Friends and Family
Subject: Marathon Training - Help

Dear Friends,

If you are a real friend, you will help me out. Next weekend my faithful running partner, Dan, is bailing on me... oops... I mean is going away for a nice long "Guys' Weekend." They rather cleverly scheduled this weekend on our first 20-miler. I will be quite honest with you, I don't know if I will be able to run 20 miles all by myself. Shit, I don't know if I'll be able to do it all.

What I need, however, is lots of support. The physical kind. I need a half a dozen friends who can run a few miles with me, then pass the torch onto some other soul willing to help me out. If you want to be part of the magic and memories, please consider running with me for a few miles. Do not be intimidated by my speed. If you can walk, then you can certainly keep up with me. I will let you know my entire route so you can hook up with me anywhere along the way. Elizabeth and Michele have kindly offered to ride a bike alongside me. That may irritate the shit out of me as I'm hunched over, gasping for air, while they pedal along giggling (and it's quite possible Michele will be drinking a martini). I would certainly lose my mind, push them off the bike, kick their asses, then take the bike and ride way. Fast.

So, for those of you who can't run, pray for me. For those of you willing to get off your fat asses and run with me... please, I beg you, can you help a sister out and run a few miles?

Love,

Steady Betty

P.S. If you don't help me, I will egg your house. And you know I will.

⌒

Date: April 24, 2009
From: Leigh Baker
To: Friends and Family
Re: Marathon Training – Journal #10

Yes, I realize I'm a little behind schedule on my journal entries, but I'm training for a freakin' marathon, people. There are some of you, namely my mother-in-law, who have serious withdrawal symptoms if I don't get a journal entry out by 3 p.m. on Sundays. Seriously, you need more entertainment in your life if this is all you have.

Last week's run was painful. I can't recall all the details. The pain, the tears, the laughs. Oh wait. There were no laughs, but the pain and tears all seem to run together. We ran 13 miles; not too daunting. After all, I ran 18 miles the week before. Hello — 18 miles! I got a little cocky and thought the 13 would be a breeze. *Not so much.* I opted for some real running shorts, circa 1979 Dolphin shorts-style. My thighs have not been so chaffed since Dan and I first started dating in 1992. The burn was unbearable. And again, I made a critical error in judgment on the bra. The nipples were sticking out several inches from my breastbone, the support was virtually non-existent, and I now believe that cotton is rotten.

Remember several weeks ago when my butt/hip/leg pain radiated down my right side? I may have perhaps overcompensated for that discomfort, and I now have serious issues with my left foot. Apparently, it's common to develop an injury on the opposite side from which your original injury began. So, not only am I dragging my right leg behind me when I walk, I am now also slightly hopping/limping on my left foot. This particular movement is almost impossible for the human body to perform, but I have perfected it to get about town.

As I said, I don't recall much from last week's run — except this one woman. She was about my age, walking along the greenway trail with a boy, approximately four years old, and dragging another boy, approximately two years old, while pushing an empty stroller and walking a dog. What caught my attention was the bottle of beer in the sippy-cup holder on the front of the stroller. This all seemed perfectly normal to me. She appeared normal in every sense — jeans, little Gap t-shirt, hair flat-ironed just so, her kids appeared clean, her dog was healthy and fat. She did not have "crazy" written on her. It was 9:30 a.m. and she was taking her kids for a morning stroll with her beer. What's wrong with that? If I weren't running, I would have introduced myself and asked for her number. We could have *so* been friends.

Anyway, blah, blah, blah... the running and all that shit. My foot was killing me all week long. I ended up calling my friend Sandy, whose husband is an Orthopedic Surgeon. By the way, I've only met this man once, and we were at a Halloween Party dressed as Deadheads. I was so drunk that I was trying to convince this man that he was, in fact, an Orthodontist, not an Orthopedic. He assured me he was not, *but I knew he was.* Anyway, I called the orthopedic guy (even if my foot hurt, surely my teeth were also going to start hurting sooner or later) and he scheduled me for an MRI. It was possible I had a stress fracture in my foot. He said, "I hate to tell you this, but if you have a stress fracture in your foot... your marathon is going to come and go and you're not going to be a part of it." *HALLELUJAH!* I mean, *Dammit.*

So after two trips to the hospital this week, and countless hours sitting in waiting rooms and little machines that looked like the space shuttle, it turned out I do not have a stress fracture. Dr. Orthopedic Surgeon/ Orthodontist Man informed me, "The E.R. said your foot is not fractured, but that it's all in your head and you're a crazy drug-seeker.'"

Let me just say, I have a legitimate relationship with a therapist and I do not need to fake illnesses to get meds. You can't fake this kind of crazy, anyway. Dr. Dentist Man did say I have a very inflamed extender tendon. I'm sure it's the biggest, most beautiful tendon he's ever seen. (Sorry, I'm about two glasses of wine into this email). So I have tendonitis in my fucking foot. I don't know what that means. He referred me to a colleague and I will see him in a week or so. In the meantime, I have prescribed myself rest and wine. So far, I'm being a very good patient to myself.

I'm slightly drunk. I don't know if it's because of the wine or the mere thought of drinking on a Friday night and sleeping in on Saturday morning. Since I've been training for the marathon, I've been unable to enjoy the vino on Friday evenings. I will be indulging this evening, sleeping in tomorrow and enjoying a pain-free weekend. I haven't skipped a Saturday run since January first. This is exactly why you should not make New Year's Resolutions on New Year's Day — they're stupid.

OK, you all enjoy your evening. I know I will.
XO,
Steady Betty

⟨⟩

Date: May 2, 2009
From: Leigh Baker
To: Friends and Family
Re: Marathon Training – Journal #11

Weather Report: 82 degrees and 50% humidity
Goal: 13 Miles

My right ass cheek is killing me.

Last week Dan was out of town for a boys' weekend, so I gave myself the weekend off. I prescribed myself lots of rest and wine. Well, now I know why I'm not a doctor; that probably wasn't the best medicine. Although the rest did feel good, the lack of running didn't do much for my official training schedule. Today I was supposed to run 13 miles, but the time off made it feel more like 20.

We ran a new route today on the American Tobacco Trail. It was really cool. Beautiful scenery, trees that provided a nice canopy of shade over the trail — a nice, long and quiet run. The Tobacco Trail is an old railroad track, so it was nice and flat with a soft surface to run on (good for the knees and feet). By far, the most beautiful trail we've been on.

It took about 20 minutes to drive out to the tobacco fields, which was plenty of time for Dan and me to argue. He told me my closet was a shit-hole, I told him to stop trying to change me. You know, the language of love. I insisted that he take responsibility for his part of our conversations/arguments (he insinuates a lot without saying much). He finally said, "You're fucking crazy. I'm not *insinuating* it. I'm actually saying it." Fucker. I told him that my iPod wasn't charged so he was going to have to talk to me for the whole three-hour run. He said, "That's enough to kill a man." Anyway, we continued this little banter to the Tobacco Trail, where we began our run.

Once again, I wore the wrong bra. Dan said, "When are you going to fucking learn? If I were you, I'd rather dig a dirty bra out of the laundry basket than wear a stupid-ass bra." That's gross. Then he said, "I'm going to get you three new sports bras for Mother's Day." Great, that's exactly what I've always wanted. A fucking sports bra for Mother's Day.

So that set the mood as we started our run. I chatted about stupid shit because I didn't have an iPod, until this couple passed us on their bikes. The woman yelled at her husband not to pass her on his bike because it scared her or bugged her or some shit. He growled back and mumbled something. At that point we noticed she had a huge fat lip and black eye. Dan said, "See? He had to smack her around a little." He thought that was so funny. I have to admit, she was pretty annoying.

Have I mentioned I hate running in the humidity? I would much rather run in 20 degrees and snow than humidity. We ran for several miles talking about how muggy it was outside, then I guess Dan ran out of topics to discuss. I wanted to talk about curtains, kids' school, the new babysitter, my bra... ANYTHING. I was bored to death. He only spoke every three or four miles when he ripped a big fart and said, "Humph. Sat on a duck." Yeah, that's fucking hysterical. Thanks for that engaging conversation. Just to irritate me, he said that after I finished this marathon, *he* would train for a marathon and make me train with him. "And we're running at my pace," he said. Yeah, right. I couldn't keep up with his pace for 100 yards, let alone several miles. I don't think he quite understands this process. I will run the marathon — then I WILL NEVER RUN AGAIN.

He was repaid for his snarkiness with bare man-chest. One thing Dan hates to see is a man running shirtless; for whatever reason, it bugs the crap out of him. Well, it was hot and there were a lot of shirtless men out there today. I don't mind it much because they're usually gay and shave their chests like Mr. Clean, but what does bother me is the hairy shirtless man. Yuck. Sweaty, hairy men. (Excuse me. I think I just threw up in my mouth a little bit.) I can't stand the sight of a sweaty, hairy man coming at me. I can't imagine if he rubbed up against me. I don't know how men play basketball and bump into each other when they're all nasty like that. That's disgusting. Anyway, there was one hairy guy, several gay guys and one just weird guy. He was, of course, shirtless, but as he ran toward us he flexed his pectoral muscles up and down like he was trying to wave at us with his man boobs or something. He looked like a stripper doing some weird trick with his man tits. I couldn't help but laugh out loud in his face.

We were nearing the end of our route when we saw a Copperhead snake right in the middle of the trail. It was about three feet long and its head was all reared up ready to strike someone. I should tell you, Dan is scared of one thing — snakes. And this one was a doozy. About a half mile later there was a big sign posted on the trail describing all the venomous snakes we might come across and to "beware." Dan will certainly have nightmares tonight (serves him right for wanting to get me a sports bra for Mother's Day). As we ran away from the snake, we kindly warned others by yelling, "SNAKE UP AHEAD," but one dumb lady with her stroller went trotting up to the snake calling, "I want to see!" Stupid bitch. Her kid is going to get bitten by a venomous snake and she'll be hauling ass back to the parking lot, screaming like a lunatic. Some people are so stupid.

I was in no shape to stop her, though, because my right ass cheek started killing me. There's some muscle in my right butt/thigh/leg that's strongly protesting this whole running thing. We're currently in a battle, and I think it may win. I stopped several times, rubbed my butt and teared up a little. I tried the whole mind-over-matter approach. I tried to scare my ass cheek into submission. It didn't work, so I alternated between walking and running the last two miles. My feet hurt almost constantly; I have blisters and calluses all over them, and I'm about five miles away from losing a toenail on my left foot. My right foot has developed an additional bone that wants to protrude out of my skin. And naturally my pedicure is beyond sad. Thank goodness I only have a few more weeks of this nonsense and then I can get back to my mochas and Cheetos.

I have an appointment on Tuesday with a second Orthopedic/Orthodontist regarding my foot. So far, no stress fracture. We'll see what the protocol is for the tendonitis they suspect I have. If I'm allowed to continue my running schedule, next weekend may be the 20-miler. Wish me luck.

Love,
Steady Betty

Date: May 9, 2009
From: Leigh Baker
To: Friends and Family
Re: Marathon Training – Journal #12

Weather Report: hot & humid
Running Goal: far

Today is Mother's Day ~ Here's a little song I made up.
    Happy Mother's Day to me
    I have aches in my knee...
    My left foot is in a boot
    Seeing me run is such a hoot
    Three weeks until the race
    If I ever think of doing this again ~ spray my face
with mace
    - Lyrics by Leigh Baker

Remember, Orthopedic/Orthodontist Man said I do not have a stress fracture in my left foot. He did, however, refer to me another dentist to check my foot for tendonitis. I saw him this week and he confirmed that I do have tendonitis, with a lot of inflammation. He also said the MRI showed I have thickening of the tendon itself. Apparently, once you have thickening of the tendon, you run the risk of rupturing it. Ruptured tendon = surgery = no marathon = no more spandex = no more chaffing = no more GU... Sorry, I got carried away. The surgery would be a bad thing, right? Anyway, Dr.

Dentist Man gave me a boot to wear on my foot for the rest of the month. He said I must wear this boot to completely rest the tendon so I don't rupture it. He also said I'm not allowed to run more than five miles at a time during the week and no more than 12 miles on Saturdays. Yay. I have to put these flexor patches on my foot every 12 hours, which dispenses some ibuprofen type crap into my tendon. And I have to go to physical therapy twice a week until the marathon. Can you believe this? I always knew exercise was a bad thing.

So Tuesday I got my fancy industrial gray boot to wear, which totally clashes with my pedicure. I'm thinking of decoupaging it with some cute Kate Spade-like paper. I hobbled around town in my boot all day, compensating with my right leg the whole time. The boot is thick and big and raises my foot up a good two inches higher, whereas my right foot is cutely outfitted with a J. Crew flip-flop, which is flush with the ground.

24 hours of limping around like I have a wooden leg proved to be a little much for my right leg. Wednesday morning I went to the gym, took my boot off to run a few miles, and hopped on the treadmill, eager to get started (or to get it over with). I ran along happily for about 45 seconds — then I felt a "pop" in my right knee. For the first time ever, surprisingly, I got to use that big red emergency shut-off switch on the treadmill. I yanked the little string attached to the red button and came to an abrupt stop.

I couldn't even walk. I felt the tendon in my right leg pop, and it was killing me. I hobbled up to the trainer's desk, where the clerk/trainer/high-school dropout reached behind my leg, felt my knee and very officially confirmed that my tendon was pulled. I went home and iced my right knee, put my boot back on my left foot and went to Starbucks for a mocha.

After a few days of taking it easy, I awoke as usual to tackle my long run — although my "long runs" are becoming shorter and shorter due to my multiple injuries. It was blissfully uneventful; my only real complaint was that I was hot and tired. I pooped out on two or three occasions and had to take a short walk-break, but other than that nothing that sent me to the emergency room.

I might have failed to mention this part over the last several months, but I typically celebrate my accomplishment with a nice cold beer upon arriving home from my Saturday runs. Yesterday was no different. We pulled into the garage, grabbed a cold beer on the way in and had another little "Cheers!" and "Good run!" moment. It was beautiful. The fact that I'm getting so close to the marathon, or the fact that my injury list is quickly growing, made me drink a few extra cold ones yesterday. I think I was about eight or nine cocktails in and thought I'd dance around and jump up and down in my boot like a lunatic. And now I can add hangover to my list of problems for today.

Three weeks from today is the marathon. Holy shit. Please start gathering your friends for the prayer vigil.
Love,
Steady Betty

Date: May 15, 2009
From: Leigh Baker
To: Friends and Family
Re: Marathon Training – Journal #13

Weather Forecast: 80 degrees and humid
Running Goal: 13 Miles

My faithful running partner, Dan, very graciously offered to do our long run today (Friday), as he'll be off golfing all weekend. It was kind of him to stay so committed to this process. I think he is getting a bit sick of it, however.

I have to let you in on our conversation this morning before our run. I crawled out of bed to join Dan in the bathroom to brush our teeth and get ourselves fresh for the world. I mentioned that I was so tired this morning, and he quickly said, "From what?" Like I couldn't *possibly* be tired, because all I do is sit around and eat bonbons all day. Well, as a matter of fact, I was up late surfing decorating websites for over four hours while he was at the bar watching a hockey game. He countered, "You know all this decorating shit isn't going to make you happy."

"Let's try it and see."

He said, "Our house is fine just the way it is. Stop redecorating it." I didn't have any coffee in my body and was ill-prepared for any snappy comebacks or justification as to why I should be allowed to redecorate, so I stomped off and pouted all the way to the coffee pot. Dan quickly followed, saying, "I'm not trying to be difficult. I just don't understand your need to redecorate."

I turned around from the coffee pot, tears streaming down my face and tried to argue, "You don't understand. It's a *feeling*. I want the house to have a certain *feeling*."

He yelled, "What the hell are you crying for?" He stood there and looked at me. If I could read his mind he was probably thinking, *Damn, this bitch is crazy. I better start stashing some cash and a change of clothes in my trunk for a quick get-a-way.*

I mumbled something like, "Just forget it," and we went on with our morning.

We dropped the kids off at school and headed out to the trail for a 13-mile run. Dan didn't say more than ten words to me the whole time. In addition to being annoyed with me, I think he's completely sick of running at my pace. Hell, I'm sick of running at my pace.

He must have run at least four more miles than me today; he'd run up about a half a mile, then circle back and catch up with me, then sprint ahead, circle back and catch up with me. He ran circles around me the entire fucking run. He was either sick of running slow with me or just trying to irritate me. Either way, he ran fast and an extra five miles and got a great work out. I, on the other hand, huffed and puffed the whole time.

I shuffled for 13 miles thinking, *How the hell can I redecorate the house?*

He ran for 18 miles thinking, *How much life insurance did I take out on this crazy bitch?*

Around mile five or six, I had to duck into a McDonald's to take a shit and blow my nose. I had snot running down my face for at least two miles — it wasn't pretty. I had on my running tank top, a great bra (finally), my kick-ass compression capris and my fuel belt around my waist. The fuel belt is essentially the thickest Velcro available on planet earth. I'm sure it was produced at NASA. So while boogers streamed down my face, I attempted to un-tuck my tank top, which had gotten stuck in the Velcro of my fuel belt. I was trying to tug on it, rip it, *anything* without tripping myself, just to pull my shirt up to my face and wipe my snotty face. Once again, I looked like a complete idiot running down the Greenway trail. Dan was miles ahead of me, completely oblivious to my fight with the shirt. (You know what just occurred to me? Perhaps he's sick of being *seen* with me, and that's why he ran so fast to-day. Oh, I'm embarrassing him, huh? Motherfucker.) Anyway, my nose continued to run all morning and ir-ritated the crap out of me.

On top of that, apparently I missed a spot on my right arm while applying Body Glide this morning. My right armpit was completely chaffed, so I began to run with my right arm as far away from my body as possible while holding my hand up in the air. I looked like I was just waiting for someone to run by and give me a high-five for, like, eight miles. (It's really becoming quite clear to me now why Dan didn't want to run next to me.) Pretty soon I'm going to have to hang out with the other trail weirdoes, like this guy I saw sitting on a rock wall, just watching the runners go by. He was about 38 years old, balding, on the shorter side. He was wearing work boots with socks pulled up to his eyeballs, shorty shorts and a red Lycra tank top that had a zipper on the front, which he'd unzipped down to his belly button. SHAZAAM! He was hot. I'm tellin' you girls, there are some real winners out on the running trail.

I made it back to the car without stopping, a rarity at this point, but I was dead tired and sweating like a pig. I thought, *Shit. If this were the marathon, I'd have 13 more miles to go.* What the fuck was I thinking? I hon-estly I have no idea how I'm going to get this done. I'm either the most determined or the dumbest person you may ever meet. I'm leaning toward the latter.

The good part, though? It's Friday, my run is done for the weekend and I can drink wine tonight. I can't remember the last time I got to drink wine on a Friday night. OK, so maybe it was last Friday. But I can seriously drink tonight.

That might have been my last long run before the Marathon. I should start to taper over the next week or so. I'm looking forward to that. Actually, I take that back — I'm not looking forward to tapering. I'm looking forward to the day the marathon is over, I sleep in on a Saturday, get up, drink tons of coffee without the thought of when, how or where I will shit that day, go straight to the couch, turn on HGTV and not think of exercising one fucking bit. That's what I'm looking forward to.

The wine is calling...

Love,
Steady Betty

Date: May 22, 2009
From: Leigh Baker
To: Friends and Family
Re: Marathon Training – Journal #14

Weather Report: 86 degrees with 46% humidity
Running Goal: 10 Miles

The marathon is fast approaching and today was definitely my last long run. I'm in the taper week of my training schedule, though my running coach informed me that since I didn't actually get in my 20-mile runs (due to injuries), I'm not really tapering from anything. Whatever. She's being a bitch right now.

It seems that my running journals have become quite popular; I've heard they've been forwarded over and over all over the planet, inducing laughter everywhere. My running coach (to whom I purposely do *not* send the journals) said she was at a dinner party with her runner friends last week (they probably all shared a salad) and someone I don't even know brought a copy of one of my journal entries. Oops. I didn't want her knowing how much I really hate running. Shit, I have to act like I have some respect for her career, right? After all, she's a fucking stud. Anyway, I was embarrassed and nervous until she confessed that she thought it was hilarious. *Phew.*

My confidence was waning on Friday afternoon, when I asked Cameron (who is 4 years old) to ride his bike alongside me so I could go for a short run. After about 300 yards he said, "Mommy, I can't ride my bike that slow to keep up with you." That little fucker. So our short run turned into him riding his bike, me trying to keep up and then us coming home after 15 minutes for a snack and a break. Now that's my idea of a workout.

But really, despite not being able to keep up with a 4-year-old on a bicycle, I have made a lot of progress. Many months ago, all this marathon training began at Lake Lynn, which is approximately two miles around. When I began this journey, I couldn't run the entire trail without stopping. It seems quite poignant that my last run was in the same place it all started — but not only can I run the entire lake now, I ran *to* the lake from our house.

Dan and I headed out of our neighborhood and down toward the lake. The streets are two-lane country roads, winding all about. Naturally, there are no sidewalks or bike lanes to be seen. We very carefully ran along the narrow road, trying to hug the grass as much as possible, hoping to not get run over by a car. A few passersby sped by, but kept a respectable distance from us. One car came awfully close to brushing up against me, and as he swerved we noticed the huge "STUDENT DRIVER" sign on top of the car. Great. I can see myself getting hit by a student driver one week before my marathon. At that moment, I realized I was in great danger running on that road. Not just running on the open road, but that I could really be hurt at any moment and ruin all my chances of running the marathon. I thought, *I don't want to take any chances, maybe I should go home and just sit on the couch until marathon day...* But we managed to survive the dangers of running down Ray Road and arrived at the lake in one piece.

By the time we got there I was, of course, sweating to death. I don't know if you've realized this yet, but I hate to sweat. It's just gross and really goes against my master plan of sitting around being lazy. It's almost impossible to break a sweat being lazy.

During our first lap around the lake, we passed two black gals who yelled, "Well, go ahead witcho bad self. We saw ya'll runnin' down Ray Road while we was drivin' to da lake!" They were so funny. We ran with them for a few hundred yards, talked about running and my fabulous compression tights. They were very impressed that I was training for the marathon and cheered me on. As we ran on ahead of them, one of the gals said, "You gotcho self a nice runnin' potna there!" I was like, "Bitch, back off my husband." Just kidding. They were very fun.

Somewhere during our second lap of the lake, we saw some weird guy striding along. His form looked like a horse stretching it out at the Kentucky Derby. His knees were coming all the way up to his chin and then stretching out a good four to five feet in front of him before he put his foot back down. Dan and I laughed as he passed us, and Dan said, "Did you see Strider Boy?" Then he proceeded to imitate him, and hurt himself — yes, Dan pulled a muscle trying to imitate Strider Boy.

So funny. Running provides so much entertainment. Who knew?

About 15 minutes later we ran into our friend, Pat. He was hauling ass, pushing his baby stroller around the lake. I was supposed to go running with Pat's wife, Colleen, the day before, but our schedules didn't work out. Turns out she was under the weather. Knowing Colleen, I figured that meant she was hung-over, so I asked Pat, "How's Colleen? Is she sick?"

He said, "She went to girls' night out dinner last night and she thinks someone slipped her a roofie." A what? Seriously? I never laughed so hard in my life. She's fine (I hope). But, seriously? Who scopes out a woman during Moms' Night Out, slips her a roofie and thinks they're going to get lucky? We moms are like a pack of geese. We stick together, cackling as loudly as we can, and not one of us is going to get away from the pack without the others knowing it. If there's a man brave enough to penetrate (no pun intended) the pack of geese, bring it on. So I'm guessing Mr. Roofie, if he existed, was unsuccessful with Colleen and one of her mommy friends escorted her home safely. It made for a humorous story. Thanks, Pat and Colleen; that got me through a couple of miles.

After a few laps around the lake, we headed back out on Ray Road, though you'd think we were running through Compton, the way I'm talking about it. About a mile or so up Ray Road, home girl from the lake pulled up alongside us, rolled down her window and yelled, "You go girl!" I was so excited to see her, like she was my long lost best friend. Dan and I waved and yelled back like we were in the marathon already. She'll never know how much that meant to me.

Running on Ray Road made me a little nervous, so I sped up a bit on the way back home. That actually turned out to be good because a few people we knew drove by and honked, so they probably thought that was my normal speed. Suckers. I was just trying to avoid getting hit by a car, but it made me look like a serious runner. I made excellent time during my run and surprised myself. Who knows, maybe I'll actually do well at the marathon.

Stayed tuned for my last pre-marathon journal entry in the next few days.

Love,

Steady Betty

Date: May 25, 2009
From: Leigh Baker
To: Friends and Family
Re: Marathon Training – Journal #15 – Reflections

This is a bittersweet email. My training has come to an end, and the marathon is just a few short days away. While I won't miss the torture of running each and every Saturday morning, I will miss these little chats. I've learned a lot about myself, and about running, over the last six months. I'll share just a few of the things I've learned, as I reflect on my experiences.

1. I hate running. OK, I didn't just learn this. I've always known this. Training for a marathon has just confirmed that little fact for me.
2. Training for a marathon is not for sissies.
3. Never underestimate the importance of a good running bra, regardless of the size of your boobies.
4. Cotton is rotten.
5. Avoid too much coffee the morning of a long run, and try to poop *before* you leave the house.
6. I should have stretched more.
7. I should have drunk more water.
8. I should have done more abdominal crunches.
9. Do not cut your hair too short to fit into a pony-tail for running.
10. Always pack extra GU.
11. You can never apply too much Body Glide.
12. Update your iPod regularly.
13. Your body is capable of much more than you give it credit for.
14. Skorts were not meant for me to run in.

15. Goose poop is very slippery.
16. It's easier to run in the freezing cold than hot weather.
17. My skin feels like sandpaper when I'm done running because of all the salt I sweat out.
18. It's impossible to run when you have a huge poop ready to come out.
19. You can, in fact, run a half marathon while starting your period.
20. There are all kinds of runners.
21. Running makes you feel free.
22. It's easier to run with a partner.
23. Running on a treadmill sucks.
24. Always put a tissue in your pocket in case you have to pee or blow your nose.
25. Some people are just born to run. I am not one of those people.
26. Extreme fatigue makes you hallucinate about Butterball turkeys.
27. Dan should not drink Amber Ale before running.
28. Wedgies are not good.
29. Veggies are not good.
30. Chaffing hurts for days.
31. Break in your new running shoes before a long run.
32. Get a fuel belt that fits correctly.
33. Always track your mileage route before running.
34. The power of prayer works.

35. Dan's left nut occasionally plays hide & seek.
36. I hate people who are too chipper when they run.
37. I hate people who can't manage to wave back at you when you pass them.
38. I hate people who hog the trail and can't move the fuck over.
39. I hate people who run with cologne on.
40. I hate girls who make it look easy.
41. Dan hates people who run without a shirt.
42. Massage therapy helps recovery.
43. Ibuprofen helps recovery.
44. Alcohol helps recovery.
45. My friends are a wonderful support system.
46. Turns out I make a lot of people laugh.
47. Compression capris rock.
48. Dan is the best running partner ever.
49. As much as I hate to admit it, it really is mind-over-matter.
50. And I hate to admit this even more; I kind of enjoyed the running.

Now that my training is over, I'm trying to just wrap my mind around the fact that I'm going to be running a freaking marathon in a few days. Some have said, "Oh, you'll be fine." Apparently, they didn't read all my journals very closely. I only made it up to 18 miles, injured myself on various occasions and cry at every mile beyond 13. Others have said, "I'll start praying for you." Those are my real friends who know me and know that the only thing that's going to carry my sorry ass is a prayer.

We fly out to California Thursday morning. My friend Kerri gave me the best advice: pack every single thing you need for race day in your carry-on bag. Brilliant. We'll arrive Thursday afternoon and settle into the time zone. Friday, I'll get in a run to get used to the weather (even though I lived most of my entire life in California, I never once ran while I lived there and have no idea what running in 68-degree perfect weather is like), map out the race, then pick up my race number and packet. On Saturday I plan to pig out at our favorite pizza shop, go to bed early and start shitting my pants. Sunday, I'll probably be out by 5:30 a.m. — the race begins at 6:30. I should be on the ambulance my 10:30 a.m., checked into the ICU by 11:30.

Well, thanks for being a part of this little sliver of my life I like to affectionately call Hell. For reading all my journals, for forwarding them to all your friends, for laughing and crying with me, for praying for me, encouraging me, for those who ran with me, offered to run with me, offered to ride a bike next to me with a martini, and for those who are inspired because of me — here's to you. I couldn't have made it this far without each and every one of you cheering me along the way. Thank you.

Stay tuned for next week's final journal entry - The Marathon.

As always,

Steady Betty

Date: June 3, 2009
From: Leigh Baker
To: Friends and Family
Re: Marathon Training – Journal #16 – The Marathon

I made it.

I can't believe I ran a marathon. Let me say that again. I ran a marathon! 26.2 miles!

We arrived in San Diego on Thursday night, and I thought I might as well start carb-loading right away; I wasn't going to let a lack of food be the reason I didn't make it! Friday morning I continued my eating extravaganza, then headed down to the Health Expo to pick up my running packet. When I entered the Convention Center I thought, *Holy shit, these people are serious. They're actually going to run this thing.* Honestly, I just showed up for a cute t-shirt and my two free beers. I showed my photo ID (I lied, I'm not 128 pounds) and they gave me my race number. I didn't immediately notice the race bib until Dan pointed out that I was supposed to fill in all the Urgent Medical Information on the back. "What's that for?" I so naively asked.

The race volunteer answered, "In case they find your body, they'll know who to call." *My body? Oh my God.* Then I had to sign a release form saying that I understood that I could die during this event. Die? *Oh my*

God, I could really die trying to run this marathon. I don't make it a habit of participating in things where there's a chance I might die. Now what am I supposed to do? Do I sign my own Death Certificate, grab my cute shirt and go on? Or do I run screaming and crying from the Convention Center like I've been set on fire?

You're damn right. I took the cute shirt and pretended I wasn't scared to death.

The Health Expo had a lot of cute things. We're talking fashion, of course. Lots of cute headbands made from the ever-lovable wicking fabric. I debated between "Run Forest Run" in a lovely forest green and "Wanna Race?" with a little green turtle embroidered on it. In the end, I opted for the beige "Marathon Mama" headband. From there I wandered over to the undergarments section to purchase a "marathong" and another cute t-shirt. (This is how bad the recession has gotten. I had to register for a fucking marathon in order for Dan to increase my wardrobe budget.) After tasting numerous things they tried to pass off as food and fuel, we left to eat Mexican food and drink more wine.

Saturday was my favorite day. This was the carb-loading day I had dreamt of since I registered for this stupid marathon. I had waited a long six months for the day I could walk into Oggi's Pizza and order everything I wanted. There was a slight setback, however; my running coach strictly forbade my favorite salad, which I had been craving. I was told to avoid lettuce, dairy and acidic foods the day before the marathon. She said nothing of Pale Ale, though. Anyway, I ate until I felt like exploding, then I ate a little more. We headed back to the hotel, where all the kids made big signs to hold up, the adults drank lots of beer and I sipped water as my impending death approached.

Sunday morning I woke up at 4:30 a.m. and thought, *What the fuck am I doing? I'm getting up to go run a marathon. Who does that?* Well, apparently, 20,000 other people did it that morning, too. Dan drove Jen and me downtown to the starting line, kissed me good-bye and reminded me to fill out the Urgent Medical Information on the back of my race number so they could get my body back to him. It was about 62 degrees and sprinkling. If there was ever a perfect day to run a marathon, this was it. Jen and I ran straight to the porta-potties to try to take a crap before the race started. Let me just say, of the 20,000 runners, about 19,000 of them were trying to squeeze out a crap at five minutes to go-time.

I can't even tell you how nervous I was. People were stretching and running and jumping and still carb-loading everywhere. There were bagels and bananas and Gatorade flying in every direction. Then I saw the "Poop High-Five." This is when you run out of a porta-potty and high-five your buddy 'cuz you managed to pinch one off before the marathon. I'm not kidding. I waited in the line for at least 20 minutes, watching all the commotion around me, wondering if I was dreaming or if I'd already died or was just about to die. It started to rain a bit more and the whispers turned into panic among the runners, but I said, "Rain? Bring it on. I trained in this shit all winter." Some weird guy behind us in the porta-potty line was chatting up my friend Jen about her estimated finish time or some crap. While they chatted about their 4-hour best, I just prayed that the next porta-potty had toilet paper.

You want to see a nasty porta-potty? Run a marathon. You think rock concerts and county fairs are nasty? No, sir. There is a lot of shit bein' had at a marathon. When it was finally my turn, I hovered over that nastarduous hole, trying to push out a poop. It was 6:28, two minutes to go-time, and I hovered and pushed and prayed while someone sang the national anthem over a loudspeaker. Just when the song was over the fireworks blasted, I pinched one off, ran out, high-fived Jen and we ran to the start line.

Based on my estimated finish time, I was assigned to Corral 18. I could barely see the starting line from Corral 18. Jen was in Corral 10. I very secretly made my way up to Corral 10 so I could start with Jen, hoping I didn't get caught and expelled from the race. Promptly at 6:30 the bell sounded and they were off — and by "they," I mean the people in Corrals 1 through 5. Several minutes passed before we got to Corral 8.

A few more minutes walking in the same direction....
"OK, we're almost to Corral 5." After several more
minutes of walking, we approached the starting line,
where we finally began running; the winner of the race
was probably already through mile four. People immediately began passing me.

What surprised me the most was the number of
people who ran in full costume. There were approximately 43 Elvis impersonators, Batman and Robin,
Nemo, Mickey Mouse, Flash, several other superhe-
roes, dozens of gay men dressed as cheerleaders, one
bear, two Teenage Mutant Ninja Turtles and much
more. Several people ran the whole marathon barefoot.
I later learned that someone ran the entire marathon
juggling four balls. Why the fuck, scratch that, *how* the
fuck do you even do that? Seriously? *Juggling?* Anyway,
all those people immediately passed me by. They were
buzzing all around; the excitement was so intense. I was
so nervous, and I swear I was tired within 200 hundred
yards. My left sock was all bunched up in my shoe already. I thought, *This can't be a good start.*

First we entered Hillcrest, which is the gay district
of San Diego. There were dozens and dozens more
gay guys dressed up as cheerleaders on the racecourse
wearing purple wigs, purple make-up, purple cheerleader outfits, and huge purple balloon boobies in their
shirts. They were hilarious. They all ran out onto the
course and high-fived people and yelled and squealed

with delight. It was very encouraging. After a few miles through Hillcrest we ran around the perimeter of the San Diego Zoo, and one of the officials announced over a loud speaker, "If this is your first marathon, you have just joined the less than 1% of the population who will run a marathon." *How cool.* At that moment I knew I was doing something big.

Around mile four I saw Dan and the kids for the first time. The kids were wearing the cute "Go Mom" t-shirts we made, holding their brightly-colored signs and yelling for me. It was awesome. Dan was beaming from ear to ear, either out of pride or maybe just because he wasn't running. Whichever it was, it brought me great joy to see his smiling face. Jen and I had already sucked down all of our Gatorade and asked Dan for a refill.

"Refills? Already? I didn't bring any yet." *What?* You have one job: bring us fuel. Shit. We agreed to meet up around mile eight, where he would be dutifully standing with our Gatorade refills. That would've been great, except we missed each other at the mile eight marker.

There were, however, Cytomax, GU and water stations sprinkled along the course. At some point we began seeing First Aid/Medic stations with volunteers handing out something that looked like a Popsicle. It was a wooden tongue depressor stick with gooey stuff on it. I grabbed one and just before I popped it in my mouth, Jen yelled, "That's not a popsicle! That's

Vaseline for chaffing." Oh. I was totally going to eat that.

The first few miles were pretty emotional. People run marathons for all different reasons. Some had shirts honoring loved ones who had passed. Some ran for their children, mothers, and fathers. Some ran to raise money to combat diseases. Some ran because they had nowhere else to wear their costumes until October. And, like me, some ran to prove something to themselves. Like warriors they painted words, scriptures and proverbs across their bodies. Some bedazzled the hell out their clothes. Some walked, some ran, some shuffled. Some laughed, some cried, some screamed and hollered the whole way. Some just ran. I think I did a little of it all.

I soaked it all in, but I think what brought me back to reality was the sound of paramedics every few minutes. After about ten miles, the sirens were getting more frequent. I didn't actually see her fall, but one girl was on the ground with a paramedic hovering over her; her face was all bloody, her arm and leg were shredded up and she was bleeding and crying everywhere. I felt terrible for her. I didn't stop though. It's a very weird marathon thing. You see people bite the dust or have a heart attack or something and you just look at them and go, "Bummer" and keep on running.

I had lots of supporters along the route. I saw my girlfriend from San Francisco, Becky, her husband, and their 9-month-old baby, Lily. They ran along with me for about 100 yards with Lily bouncing in the Baby Bjorn. It was great. Around mile 12 I saw my parents, my sister and her boyfriend (common law husband by California standards — she already gets half) their kids, and my uncle Chip. They all held up their signs, screamed and hollered for me. It was awesome.

Right after that I saw Nordstrom's, and I considered popping in there to see if their Half Yearly Sale was still going on. Some shopping would've been so much more enjoyable than running; I was starting to get really tired. I didn't realize there was a Half Marathon going on at the same time, so imagine my jealousy when thousands of people stopped at mile 13, celebrated with their families and they were done. *What?* I ran by the mile-13 marker/celebration station like it was a horrible car accident, and I couldn't help but stare. I was so tired and thought, *Oh shit, I have 13 more miles to go.* That's when I considered crying.

The rest was a blur. Jen suddenly turned into "Chipper Jen" and I thought I was going to punch her in the face. She ran along, cheerfully yelling, "Are you in the zone? Let me know when you're in the zone and we can just cruise. Are you in the zone, yet?" What the fuck *zone* is she talking about? Yeah, I'm in the I-wanna-stop zone. She ran backwards in front of me saying, "You're doing great, Leigh!" Seriously? Running backwards? Was that necessary? I must've looked like her charity case. At one point she jumped off the course and ran into a Starbucks to go pee. As she trotted off in her cute little shorts (bitch) she yelled, "Don't stop, I'll catch up with you." Of course she'd catch up with me; I was only about 50 yards ahead when she got out of the bathroom. I think that was the best part of the run for her, picking up her pace to catch up with me. Don't get me wrong, I am so grateful for Jen. Apparently, her normal race time would be around four hours, but she had to run super slow to stay back with me and encourage me the whole way. That must have been brutal, but I'm eternally grateful. I still wanted to punch her in the face though. She's so darn skinny and cute and positive it made me want to hit her. After she turned into Chipper Jen I said, "Do you mind if I ask Dan for my iPod when we see him next? Because you're kinda getting on my nerves now." She didn't mind at all; in fact, she was probably thinking, *Oh thank God. I don't how much longer I can drag your sorry ass along.* When I got my iPod, I definitely sped up a lot. Probably almost to an *actual* run. I knew Jen was happy.

I think I hit a wall around mile 18 or so. Apparently I saw Dan and the kids at that point, but I don't recall. Dan said Jen ran up ahead of me and told him, "I think she's OK." He ran out on the course, I kissed him as I kept running but didn't speak a word. He yelled, "Do you need anything? More Gatorade? Snacks?" Jen answered for me, "I think she's OK." I just kept running.

I don't remember any of that. Dan said that's when he started to get worried. He said I looked so bad that, for the first time, he thought he might go home a widower. Ambulance sirens were screaming everywhere and I stumbled off into the sun in a complete fog. He wondered if he'd ever see me again. I'm sure it was a bittersweet moment for him.

Somewhere around mile 21, I saw Becky again. Her husband and the baby were asleep in the car along the side of the road, so she caught up with Jen and me and ran along with us for a good mile or so. *Thank you, Becky.* I don't think I spoke one word to her, but I appreciated it so much. Bless her heart — she tried so hard to communicate with me, encourage me and cheer me on, but I just kept running in a complete daze. Becky is not a runner; she was breathing louder than I was, her face was beet red and she was already sweating to death after 25 yards. But she was doin' it. Go Beck. She was on her cell phone the entire time, reporting back to Dan that I was, in fact, still alive, although unresponsive. She tried to coordinate various points for him to see me again, which was incredibly helpful due to my inability to speak.

The last few miles were the loooooongest. I cranked up my iPod as loud as I could and just kept running. Chipper Jen advised, "As we get close to the finish line, turn your iPod off so you can soak it all in." I gave her a thumbs up because I couldn't speak, thanks to the exhaustion and nausea; I had carb-loaded, eaten about 8 GUs, guzzled Gatorade, scarfed down pretzels, Fig Newtons, salt packets and one Vaseline pop. I thought I was going to throw up. I hoped I had enough fuel in my body to get me through the last hour, because there was no way I could eat or drink one more thing. It's quite possible that I gained weight running this marathon.

The crowds were increasing, the cheers were getting louder and louder, the bands were jamming. I turned off my iPod and just kept going. The finish line was inside the Marine Corps Recruiting Depot on base, so as we entered the military base we were greeted by marines lined up, cheering, clapping and giving us high-fives. I wanted to stop and tell them, "Thank you. *You're* the ones who have done something great, not me."

As I approached mile 26 all the fans were yelling, "Oh my God, there's a guy running and juggling behind you. Look! Look! Turn around!" At first, I thought they were just fucking with me, trying to get me to turn around so I'd fall right there and kill myself. I was slightly irritated that they'd do that. The farther we ran, the more fans kept hollering, "Oh my God, there's a juggler!"

Jen, who was way more coordinated and less tired than me, turned around while running and said, "Hey, there *is* a juggler running behind you."

At the 26 Mile Marker I decided to full-out sprint (an easy jog for most). I just turned it on and went for it. Two tenths of a mile to go, and I just wanted this stupid thing to be over. Soon, I saw my whole family in the bleachers right next to the finish line, yelling and screaming for me. *It was awesome.* Jen grabbed my hand; we raised our arms in the air like Thelma and Louise and just hauled ass. Then I remembered they take your photo as you cross the finish line so I dropped Jen's hand, raised my arms above my head, gave the double peace sign, and screamed, "WAHOO!" as loud as I could as I finished the race.

It was glorious.

About 25 yards later, my legs finally stopped. I bent over like I was going to throw up and a paramedic jumped out of nowhere and said, "Are you OK? Do you need a medic?"

"No, I think I'm OK."

He said, "You wouldn't be the first one to puke on me today." How encouraging.

I remember pushing him out of my way and wandering off. People handed me water and bananas and more food; this was basically a big food fest with some running thrown in. I stumbled over to some ladies who congratulated me and put a medal around my neck. Jen and I posed for a quick photo, then stumbled toward more food tables. It took about ten minutes to wander through the buffet to get to our families. Up until then I was just exhausted, but when I saw Dan I burst into tears.

"I did it. I really did it."

I couldn't believe I'd really done it. I ran the whole thing without stopping. The kids hugged me, my parents rushed over to congratulate me, I think my sister was crying. It was so surreal. This was better than Mother's Day, my birthday and Christmas combined. I just kept mumbling, "I did it. I ran the whole thing without stopping."

After about 30 minutes of standing there in complete shock, my family started comparing stories about seeing me and other runners. Everyone saw the Running Elvis, the juggler, the gay cheerleaders, and Nemo. They told me about a man who sprinted across the finish line completely naked except for a cape and a helmet. They talked about people throwing up or crying uncontrollably as they finished. The funniest one seemed to be the old man who finished just before me, pushing an oxygen tank. That's right, he finished before me. I thought, *If that old man is in my finish line photo, I'll be so fucking pissed.*

After listening to stories for a while I said, "OK, this is fun and all, but I'm done. I've gotta go lie down now." I cannot begin to describe to you how sore I was. I have never been so sore and tired in all my life, but we still had to walk about a mile to the car. They should really have valet at a marathon. Why has no one thought of this? I tiptoed back to the car and finally sat down for the first time in over seven hours. I let out the biggest sigh you've ever heard, and then ordered Dan to take me to In-And-Out for a big, juicy burger.

After the marathon and burger, I went straight to the hotel Jacuzzi to soak. That was nice, until my little Calgon moment was interrupted by six 20-year-olds wondering how they were going to score some beer. I was like, "I will buy each of you a shot and a case of beer if you just get lost." That didn't work. I think the challenge of using a fake ID was more exciting to them.

After my long, semi-relaxing soak I took a four-hour nap, but I continued to get more and more sore by the minute. I swear my feet were bloody stumps on the bottom of my legs. My left foot had three huge blisters, one toenail was hanging on by a thread, another one was black and it felt like I had walked over hot coals for six hours. A three-time Iron Man competitor in the pool had told me an Epson Salt bath would solve a lot of my problems, so Dan ran out and got me the Oggi's chopped salad that I was unable to consume the day before the marathon and some Epson salt. I love that man. I inhaled that salad like nobody's business. After the Epson Salt bath, I went back to bed. Ahhh...

Jen called me later that night to see how I was feeling. I said, "I'm so sore. I can't move. I think I'm going to die. How are you feeling?"

Chipper Jen chirped back, "My knees are a little sore, but they'll be OK 'cuz I have a tennis match in the morning." Seriously, what the fuck is wrong with her?

She also told me that her friend, Cliff from KSON's *Cliff & Company* radio show in San Diego, had heard about my Steady Betty journals and wanted to interview me on the radio.

They called me the next morning.

Cliff: We had the Rock and Roll Marathon yesterday, and the weather would have been perfect for running that kind of distance. Leigh ran the marathon. They call her Steady Betty. Leigh, how ya doing? How'd you make out?

Leigh: (laughter) I did good.

Cliff: Have you ever run a marathon before?

Leigh: No, and I will never run one again, in case you're wondering.

Cliff: So what was your time then? Because that's the big thing: your time, right?

Leigh: No. Actually the big thing is not dying.

Cliff: (laughter)

Leigh: But my time was 5 hours and 47 minutes.

Cliff: But you finished.

Leigh: I ran the whole thing and did not stop.

Cliff: Good for you. Well, what an accomplishment.

Leigh: I know. It's crazy.

Cliff: Well, it was yesterday. So how are you feeling this morning?

Leigh: I'm sore as hell.

Cliff: I bet. (laughter) I bet. Are you taking today off? You have stuff to do? What's your plan?

Leigh: My husband scheduled a massage for me. I'm sitting around on my butt doing nothing...
Cliff: (laughter) Good for you. Well, you sound in good spirits. You should be proud of yourself.
Leigh: I am. It's crazy. I cannot believe I did that.
Cliff: And to everyone who ran, walked, crawled, huffed their way through, whatever it took to accomplish what is truly a lifetime accomplishment for anybody who makes it through a marathon — well done.

Friends called to say, "I just heard you on the radio!" That was so funny. I'm a rock star.

OK, so the question on everyone's mind: Will I ever run a marathon again? My answer: HELL NO. I'm so glad I did it. My goals were to 1) not die, 2) run the whole thing, and 3) run it in five hours. So, two out of three isn't bad, especially since it was the best two of the three options.

Running the marathon was by far the hardest thing I've ever done in my entire life. I have no desire to ever do it again, but I proved to myself that I can do anything. Running this marathon has changed my life — I feel like a completely new person. I ran a freaking marathon, people! That's fucking awesome.

For those of you who are familiar with my flying phobia (getting oxygen rolled out for me, peeing on myself, throwing up on each flight, being hypnotized), I want you to know something: Tuesday morning when we were at the San Diego Airport getting coffee to fly home, I leaned over to Dan and said, "I don't think I'm going to take my flying medicine."

He said, "Oh shit. Here we go." But I thought, *I just ran a marathon. I can do anything now.* So I skipped the Ativan and flew home — without meds or alcohol. That is huge for me. I did great, with no soiling myself, crying or puking.

I'm telling you, I'm a new person.

But I will still never run again.

As always,

Steady Betty

P.S. Guess what I'm doing next Saturday? Nothing, bitches.

Thirteen

I Get By With A Little

Help From My Friends

*I*n my next life, I'm coming back as a lesbian. Well, more specifically, a lesbian with a hysterectomy. Not because I want to smack the cooter or anything, although I suppose I'd try anything just once, but rather because eliminating men and periods just seems like the simpler way to go through life. Don't get me wrong, I'm sure the bumper-to-bumper canoodling is fantastic what with all those bouncing breasts and delicious smelling conditioner, but the female companionship is what I'm really after. Girls just *get* girls.

If I had one wish for Dan (no, it wouldn't be that he had a vagina), it'd be for him to have a sister. So, theoretically, yes I guess I do wish he had a vagina, but a sister-vagina. He simply doesn't *get* girls. Of course, he *can* get a girl — he's gotten quite a few, including me — but he doesn't *get* them. I'm convinced that if he'd sprouted up with a sister or two he wouldn't look at me with that perplexed look on his face so often. You know the look, the one that subtly implies *What the fuck is wrong with you?* He would recognize the difference between cream, ivory and off-white, how crying can be good, the necessity for five pairs of black shoes, the point of sleeping with the ceiling fan on high while also sleeping beneath eight blankets and, for God's sake, that finding a good hairdresser is a pivotal life experience. On the other hand, it wouldn't matter if Dan had had ten sisters, since there are certain things he'll never comprehend. Like why girls open their mouths wide to put on mascara, or why we strategically hide our panties in the gynecologist's office even though she's going to be looking right up our hoo-ha, or why we cough ferociously when pooping in public so that other women don't hear us drop a deuce.

Women know precisely what other women *think* and *mean*.

There have been multitudes of books and movies hatched about the significance of girlfriend relationships and the unbreakable bond between women. Sure, women can be cold and catty at times, but we value our authentic friendships more than anything and we'll hang on to a BFF longer than a way-too-small pair of jeans tucked in the corner of our closet. We treasure our giggly, drunken, soul-baring, bosom-buddy *Beaches* moments. Bette Midler speaks to women everywhere when she croons, "You can live without love, but you've got to have friends."

Having a Best Friend Forever with whom you can laugh and cry and share a severed-heart necklace is a precious thing indeed. Truthfully, it's your most devoted girlfriends who get you through the toughest and most challenging moments in life. It's not your loving husband or even your doting mother. It's your best girlfriend who will pick you up when you're down, come running with the tissues and wine when you're weepy, hold your hair back when you're vomiting or laugh with you when you take a tipsy tumble into a serene spa and giggle as you bark and flop around like a wet seal. It's your gal pal who'll understand the bittersweet end to breastfeeding, the tearful first days of Kindergarten drop-off and the agonizing immunization appointments. She'll lie on a steamy bathroom floor with you when your first-born has croup, or deliver casseroles to your door when your family contracts lice or hand-foot-mouth disease. She'll be there for the deaths of your grandmother, hamster and vibrator — each equally traumatic, in its own way — and nobly attend the funerals for all. Your BFF will be the first call you make about the proposal, the pregnancy, the divorce and the breast cancer. She'll accept your deepest, darkest secrets and encourage your biggest, boldest dreams.

It's critical to find a community of sidekicks who accept your healthy dose of crazy, share your however-absurd sense of humor and allow you the freedom to *really* be yourself. It also helps if they drink the same kind of wine as you. I have found my particular tribe of playmates who do just that; they love me in spite of myself, appreciate my foolishness, lift me up and allow me to embrace my crazy side. They are my best friends, pillars of support, and I get by with a little help from them all.

It's the little things we appreciate and adore the most in love-struck friendships such as ours. Little things like a timely invitation for afternoon wine (*Wow! Is it 3 o'clock already?*), or leaving a fine Spanish vintage of *Bitch* red wine on your girlfriend's porch for talking you into that God-awful bikini wax, or worse yet, waking up to find your own panties in your mailbox after another crazy Moms' Night Out. From sleeping on your girlfriend's sofa so she can rush to her dying father's bedside to pinky swearing to delete every naked photo from last night's party, we girlfriends stick together through it all. And in this modern world of social technology, that *little thing* that gets me through the day often comes in the form of a playful, knee-slapper text message from a dear friend.

Glass Half Full

BFF: I'm miserable. I have my period and a cold.
ME: You could have a baby and mastitis!
BFF: Always looking on the bright side!

A Sense of Style

BFF: It would be very unfortunate for real world people to think they can dress like the models in the Anthropologie catalog!
ME: R U Kidding? I wear that shit to Target ALL the time! As a matter of fact, I'm looking for the perfect, jeweled bird hat to wear.
BFF: OMG! Remember the time that other shopper had on the same purple fedora, black watch, plaid dress and orange shoes as you?
ME: Yeah. I slashed her tires with my golden owl ring!
BFF: LOL! Just snorted I'm laughing so hard!
BFF: BTW, I got drunk again last night. We need to turn this neighborhood into a rehab center.
ME: Cuz' if we don't, we're headed for The Biggest Loser instead of Project Runway.
BFF: Seriously. And I fear they'd make me wear the brown shirt. That's a horrible color on me.
ME: I'll be pissed if they put me in orange. I'd look like a huge fucking pumpkin!
BFF: Better than a big, brown turd.
ME: Tru dat.

It's All About The Hair

BFF: I have no tolerance for Starbucks virgins chattin' it up with the employees today.

ME: Look here, Bitch. Give me my Grande, non-fat, extra-hot Lexapro Latte and nobody gets hurt.

BFF: You damn right. Some young, smiley girl in bad clothes and her friend must have spent at least 3 minutes discussing what they *might* like to drink with the employee. Dude, I've got a hair appointment. MOVE ON!

ME: Oh no she d'int hold you up for a hair apt! Gasp!

BFF: I told her "C U Next Tuesday!"

ME: You're so clever.

BFF: I know. I'm so clever.

Surprise

BFF: How did your kids do on first day of school? I spent the whole day thinking about poor Cameron's meltdown.

ME: Fine. Kids were fighting all morning and not listening to me so I said, "I put a surprise in the mailbox. First one there gets to have it!" They went running outside and I locked them out of the house so I could enjoy this cup of coffee. They are crying and Dan is mad. Happy Sunday!

BFF: LOL! I LOVE IT! Another great day in the burbs!

ME: Livin' the dream, baby. Livin' the dream.

Oh, Shit

(after telling BFF I took two laxatives, three Gas-X, two Benefiber and drank four cups of coffee)

ME: As Winnie the Pooh says, "There's a rumbly in my tumbly!"

BFF: I hope you packed a change of clothes for work today!

ME: Didn't think of that.

BFF: Want me to run you over a pack of Depends.

ME: No. So far, so good. Good thing I didn't stop for a Mocha today.

BFF: UR ass is gonna make its own mochas today!

ME: Ha! Ha!

later

ME: Uh-oh.

BFF: Just in case u r wondering, North Carolina is not expecting any earthquakes today...that is ur bowels talking.

ME: My boss is back! I just blew up the bathroom. I'm going to blame it on that hot chick in the accounting office.

BFF: Smart move. Might want 2 formulate ur story for why u have to leave a smidge earlier than expected today.

ME: I need some Imodium. Can you bring me some?

BFF: And Depends! U need Depends!!

later

ME: I'm at home now. Pooping. Don't call me.

BFF: I don't think you've ever done anything that made Dan's frat boy employees feel so at home in ur house ....a stinky bathroom might bring a tear to their eyes!
ME: I think that shit was stuck in there since 1986. It had leg warmers on!

later

ME: On my way back to work now. Just gonna say.... there is a really hot guy in the car next to me at this stop light. It's hard to look sexy when u got diarrhea.

Rip

ME: Well, we knew it was coming. I officially broke my vibrator.
BFF No.1: So sad!
ME: I know. I need to pull myself together. Can you girls make funeral services on Friday?
BFF No. 1: Anything to support you during this difficult time.
BFF No. 2: Yes, but I think we need a New Orleans style funeral. We need a marching band and a parade!
ME: I love you guys.

Menopause

BFF: Right before my period starts these days, I feel like my body could internally combust at any moment. If this isn't the beginning of peri-menopause I fear the real thing!

ME: I fear that menopause for me will be somewhere between the creepy guy in Beetlejuice and the crazy bitch in Fatal Attraction who boils the rabbit.
BFF: Yikes.

Dieting

BFF: OK, I've tried out being fat. Don't think I'm enjoying this anymore.
ME: Yeah, that is so 2011. I've tried being sober and that's not working either.
BFF: Let's be anorexic drunks. Or how about bulimic coke addicts?
ME: Why don't you just put your hand in a blender? That would be less painful. And I can't afford cocaine, but I can be an anorexic drunk with you. And I don't want to be bulimic 'cuz that shit ruins your teeth.
BFF: True and shit might get caught in my braces and look nasty.
ME: Would it be crossing our friendship barrier for you to reach up my ass and put a ring around my large intestine?
ME: Pee just came out, huh?
BFF: HAHAHAHAHA!!!

Mother in-Laws

BFF: I heart Cameron.
ME: What's he doing?

BFF: Just being himself. I just like that he's a nice kid. Way to go, Leigh!

ME: That was such a mother-in-law thing to say.

BFF: You're raising nice children. Too bad you put those curtains in the den though. *That's* a MIL thing to say!

ME: No. You're raising wonderful children and we all know it comes from my perfect son and not your fucked up trailer trash family dear. Now pass your bland mashed potatoes.

BFF: And pull your skirt down a bit, you look like a streetwalker.

ME: Your son would know.

Parenting

ME: Hey Cam has homework, give us a few extra minutes then you can come down and go swimming. Felicity is trying to get out of soccer practice, which we forbid, because she has so much homework too.

ME: We "forbid" it. Because we're such perfect parents – that's what I was trying to get across. Did u get that?

BFF: As if you have to explain that you're perfect….we all know it!

ME: Just wanted to make sure. Oh, my bevy of choice today is capt and coke. It's hotter than a witch's tit in a brass bra out there and I can't be drinking wine.

ME: And I will be in my bikini. Don't judge me.

Neighborhood Parties

BFF: It was a fun night! Thanks! I swear the rain adds to the fun!

ME: Do you remember putting an entire bottle of wine in between your boobs and drinking it with a straw?

BFF: Yes ma'am. Know what's pitiful? I wasn't even that drunk.

Meals

BFF: Ordered pizza. Cam wants to eat with us. Can he?

ME: That lil' fucker! No! He asked me to cook his favorite meal and I did. Dan and Felicity are out. I am not eating his favorite meal by myself. Send his ass home!

BFF: LOL! OK.

Beer

BFF: You home

ME: No, at lacrosse.

BFF: Dan?

ME: Here with me. What's up?

BFF: Beer

ME: Front door is unlocked.

BFF: Oh perfect. Thanks for the invitation to rob your fridge!

ME: Leave nachos.

Pms

BFF: Do you find it alarming that to indulge my raging premenstrual cravings for salt and sweet, I just dipped a tortilla chip into the cookie dough?
ME: Yum

Drunk & Depressed

ME: I want to have an affair with Nate Berkus!
BFF: LOL! That gay thing might get in the way.
ME: No one has mentioned my birthday at all! I haven't been my usual pushy self about advertising it either. 41 is going to suck dick. And Felicity drew a family photo today and made me twice as big as Dan! WTF?!?!
BFF: LOL! Did she also make you have an afro and long blue dress?
ME: No. Just fat. With a big fat kindergarten crayon. Did I mention I started my period yesterday? I could eat a guacamole hot fudge sundae right now.
BFF: I'm so premenstrual I'd share that sundae with you.
ME: I feel like a crack addict. I'm sitting in my living room alone. No lights on, no T.V., no music, nothing at all. Just gulping wine and with each swig I close my eyes and sigh a little happy noise. Have you ever just sat in the dark and drank by yourself? Peaceful or pathetic?
BFF: Depends. Day two of your period, no kids or husband all up in your grill = peaceful. Large block party in front of your house, five different medications required to keep you functioning, you and your newborn baby locked in the house together = pathetic.

ME: I'm going to be the drunkest mom at soccer to-night. And this new lamp I bought from Target today looks like something Fred Flintstone would clobber Wilma with.

BFF: We all have our areas of expertise!

ME: What the fuck does that mean?

BFF: If you flip it upside down it could be a Bedrock Microphone.

ME: Oh, totally!

BFF: It means we're good at drinking and I want you to hold your drunk head up high tonight, soccer mom!

ME: Have you ever wondered if your husband would take care of you if were in a horrible car accident and were wheelchair bound? And do you think our husbands would refill our wine if we were disabled? I mean we'd have straws so they wouldn't have to hold the glass.

BFF: I discerned long ago that you and my mother would be my caretakers. I know what's up in my marriage.

ME: Do you think Nate Berkus would take care of me?

BFF: Wait! If sex were still possible our husbands would be more motivated. But Nate and his partner would be all over it!

ME: Funny! Dan just walked downstairs and I asked him if he'd take care of me if I were paralyzed and he said yes then he'd "lay me out once a week for sex." That's disgusting! The thought of him having sex with my motionless body....wait....that's what he does now....

BFF: Keep drinking. It will become less appalling.

Merry Fucking Christmas

BFF: Can I just be tacky and ask you if our children need to exchange gifts?

ME: Can I be even more tacky and say "no."

BFF: Perfect.

ME: Merry Fucking Christmas.

BFF: You forgot to put Whore at the end of that!

ME: Whore.

BFF: What'd you get for me though?

ME: A t-shirt that says, "I'm a Whore."

BFF: A big sign for my front porch that says, "This here's the house!!" By the way, girl in Trans AM ahead of me in bank line is CHECKIN her look. A lot!

ME: Das right! She got some Aqua Net in her purse and is ready to hit the town.

BFF: With her heavy black eyeliner at 1 in the afternoon.

ME: So? Whores gotta Christmas shop too.

BFF: LOL!

Donut Holes

ME: I'm at a coffee shop writing and there are two grown men (like 30-ish) sharing a plate of donut holes and playing checkers. WTF?

BFF: Go sit at their table and get all breathy and be like "are you two luvahs?" while you point your finger at them and then around in circles. And then eat one of their donut holes!

ME: I'm laughing so loud! Coffee is coming out of my nose and people are staring!
BFF: Are you at Sola?
ME: Yep, why?
BFF: 'Cuz I need a visual.
ME: They just left. Probably to make luuuuuvvvvvv!
The owner of Sola Coffee walks over and says, "Excuse me. Do you have a friend you'd like to share these donut holes with?"
"What? No," I falter.
"Are you sure? You don't have a friend or a luvah you want to share these hot donuts with?" he presses.
I say, "No. I'm good. Thank you." He leaves the donuts and walks away.
Me: OMG!! The owner just brought me two donut holes!!! I can't stop laughing!
In walks BFF, screaming, "I called and sent the donuts over to you, you idiot!!!"

Alcoholics
Me: I'm so hung-over. We need to stop drinking.
BFF: I know. I can't keep abusing my body like this.
later
ME: Is your power out too?
BFF: Yes. It's making me want to drink 'cuz I can't cook.
ME: I'm kind of bored.
BFF: I know. We have to be strong!

ME: These cookies you sent over are yummy.
BFF: Thanks. Almost a casualty – another minute and they would have been charcoal.
ME: It tastes good with this wine!
BFF: Are you?!?!
ME: No!
BFF: I think the only reason I'm not drinking is because I don't have an open bottle. Power!!!
ME: Phew!! We made it through the power outage without drinking!
BFF: We rock!!
ME: We should celebrate!!
BFF: Yes. Maybe just a beer. Beer doesn't count.
ME: Ha ha! I'm going to try not to. It's Monday for God's sake! We can do this for one night!

Having a network of cherished friends is fantastic, but let's be honest, they can't prescribe you narcotics when you need them. Sometimes life hands you shit that, frankly, a bottle of wine and a good laugh alone simply can't fix. A good friend can, however, refer you to a reputable psychiatrist!

The thing about being diagnosed *crazy* at an early age is that you can quickly identify when things get out of whack within your body. With things like neurotransmitters and shit bouncing around in your brain, it can be difficult to discern when you feel relatively normal versus marginally unbalanced. But for someone like me — being that I'm only semi-crazy and possess a precarious ability to artfully hide my nuttiness — I can, in fact, recognize when I'm OK, when I've hit rock bottom and when to ask for help.

One of my dearest friends introduced me to Dr. Miller shortly after I moved to North Carolina. I was depressed and felt isolated in an unfamiliar city with two small children looking to me for comfort and reassurance. In my distressed state, I turned to Dr. Miller for counsel and solace. I immediately loved him. He spoke softly, listened attentively, was generous with scripts and looked just like Santa Claus!

His eyes, how they twinkled, his dimples how merry. His cheeks were like roses, his nose like a cherry. His droll little mouth was drawn up like a bow and the beard of his chin was as white as the snow. The stump of a pen he held tight in his teeth and the notes he inscribed resembled a wreath. He had a broad face and a little round belly that shook when he laughed, like a bowlful of jelly! He was chubby and plump, a right jolly old elf and I laughed when I saw him, in spite of myself. A wink of his eye and a twist of his head soon gave me to know I had nothing to dread. He spoke not a word, but went straight to his work and filled my prescription then turned with a jerk. And laying his finger aside of his nose and giving a nod, off the sofa he rose. He sprang to his feet, let out a small whistle and escorted me out for a timely dismissal. But I heard him

*exclaim, as I drove out of sight, "Take this, my dear, you'll
sleep well tonight!"*

Over the course of eight years, Dr. Miller faithfully counseled me through heartache and depression. We talked about adolescence, parenting,
marriage, anxiety and phobias — even the fucking
FBI! Where other therapists focused on inkblot images and wave machines, Dr. Miller unearthed the
truth that allowed me to move from feeling deeply
sad and wrecked to feeling clear and empowered. He
challenged me, held me accountable and accepted
me for who I was. There were days when I couldn't
formulate coherent words because I cried so forc-
ibly, and even more days when I vomited more swear
words than verbs. But even during the most terrible
days, he reminded me, "You are so worthy, amazing,
resilient and lovely."

I believed him.

Sometimes.

It was uncomfortable and painful, but necessary to
the process of ridding my mind of the clutter I'd become
used to. For the first time in my life, I felt in control of
my cognitive mind and destiny. Through Dr. Miller's
guidance, I was able to see that I am not defined by others' mistakes, ill-fated circumstances or even my own
negative perception. I absorbed all that he imparted,
allowing me to interrupt my trend of negative thoughts
and neurotic template, choose my rightful path and

most importantly, believe that, despite my messy self, I deserve love.

And love me, he did. OK, maybe he didn't *love* me as much as I loved him. He was my biggest cheerleader; he believed in me wholeheartedly when I could barely decipher a butterfly from a wine stain on the inkblot test. I thought I'd narrowed down the red ink to it's vineyard and vintage when he conceded that it was neither a butterfly nor a wine stain, but a close-up of Al Gorbechev's port-wine birth mark. Well, I had the wine part right anyway.

Dr. Miller told me I was his favorite patient. Or did he say *flagrant* patient? I can't remember. The doctor-patient lines grew very blurry when Dr. Miller developed a brain tumor and I felt more like the *doctor* and he felt more like the *patient*. His practice slowed down quite a bit amidst his weakened state, leaving allowance for only a few sporadic psychiatry appointments. You can bet I snatched those scarce engagements right up, hoping my incessant griping hadn't negatively contributed to the tumor in any way. Nevertheless, I faithfully continued to meet with him up until his brain surgery.

Dr. Miller survived the invasive brain surgery, but not without severe complications. Although the tumor was successfully removed, his vocal cords were compromised, leaving him virtually speechless. He could no longer formulate words, speak or verbally communicate in any audible, comprehensible way. Although his psychiatry practice would surely have to dissolve in order to prolong his life, I was not ready to let go of my relationship with him.

The first time I visited Dr. Miller in the hospital, he was a mere skeleton of his former jolly self. His cheeks were not rosy, his nose not a cherry, his face no longer broad and not a thing was round, not even his belly. But when I leaned over his bedside like a fairy, his eyes how they twinkled, he was surely still merry! His parched little mouth turned up in a grin and I could swear he asked, "How have you been?"

"Well, I'm glad you asked," I immediately said and scooted him over in his hospital bed. I started right in with the kids and then Dan while his eyes studied the room with a cursory scan. Then on to my mother-in-law and the damn FBI, and after an hour, my plans for the Fourth of July. He smiled and nodded just like I remembered and I thought, "I better schedule September!" However, before I left I noticed the sign — it hung above his bed, shouting in bright red ink, "DON'T TALK TO THIS SHRINK."

The sign warned of absolutely no talking. It wasn't clear if Dr. Miller's voice and speech would ever be restored, and it was imperative that he not strain his vocal cords by even *attempting* to communicate. Once I observed the sign, I noticed there was a pen and paper on his nightstand should he need to communicate anything urgently. I had recently withdrawn from my two antidepressants, so luckily I didn't require a prescription refill. I tidied his room, arranged a blooming bouquet and read aloud the card I brought him — all just to enjoy his company.

Once I'd finished nervously busying myself in Dr. Miller's room, I finally pulled up a chair, took his hand in mine and sat quietly thanking God that this man saved my life. As I looked into his sweet blue eyes, it dawned on me: *My children have a mother because of this man, my husband still has a wife and I have my dignity all because this one man believed in me.* I gratefully wept at his bedside for the courage and wisdom be bestowed upon me.

Once it was time to go, he motioned for me to come toward him. A single hospital sheet covered his frail body as I held a Styrofoam cup and straw to his mouth. When I removed the straw from his pink, pursed lips, he motioned me closer. He wanted to say something. I put my ear as close to his mouth as I could. He tried to formulate his thought into an audible sound, but nothing came out. He tried again. I could feel the warmth of his breath on my ear while he tried to say something to me. He finally spoke one delicate word.

"M..m…milk…milksh..milkshake," he fought to get out.

"You want a milkshake?" I eagerly asked.

He confirmed by nodding his head and then motioned to the pen and paper on his nightstand. He
wrote in a child-like manner: *Char-Grill.*

"Oh! You want me to bring you a Char-Grill milkshake?" I enthusiastically guessed.

He nodded.

"Oh! I can do that! What flavor?" I asked him.

He started to inscribe a *V* on the paper when I pre-
emptively shrieked, "Vanilla?!"

He smiled and nodded.

"OK! I'll bring you a large, vanilla milkshake from
Char-Grill next time," I said, relieved that I understood
his request and also that I could come back to visit him.

"I'll see you next Tuesday at our regular time, Dr.
Miller!"

It was months before Dr. Miller regained his speech.
Although he wasn't technically *counseling* me during
those visits, he still provided care and friendship to me.
I faithfully fed him milkshakes, ice-chips and chicken
casseroles, all the while hoggishly chattering on and
on about my own concerns and happenings. Since he
couldn't actively protest, I assumed he didn't mind the
company and maybe even enjoyed my visits. The nurs-
es must have thought I was his devoted daughter, based
on the way I made myself at home in his room. Had he
been able to speak he might have clarified that with the
nurse, or initiated a restraining order against me. But I
wasn't quite ready for our professional relationship to

end — plus I had a few loose emotional ends I needed to tie up. I felt guilty not paying him during that time and I often wondered if I should leave a co-pay on this bedside table or just keep paying him in milkshakes.

Dr. Miller is healthy now and from time to time I pop by his home (I found his address on some county tax records) to see how he's doing. We're working on me not feeling so guilty about getting free counseling during his hospitalization.

I look back on my time at New Life, the rehabilitation hospital for teens, when I thought, *I'm nothing like these people.* Now, I realize that I am *exactly* like those people — unbreakable and resilient, brave and spirited, precious and valuable — and finally believe that I'm going to be OK. I found some old scrunchies while cleaning the other day and threw them away. I don't need them anymore; I've got my friends. Just as I sit here thinking about how I get by with a little help from my friends, my phone *dings!*

BFF: Hey, what's up?
ME: You may want to rinse out your bathtub. I peed in it last night.
BFF: U crazy!
ME: Is it showing again?

In Loving Memory of
Dr. Miller

19617897R00184

Made in the USA
Middletown, DE
28 April 2015